Fire Truck Toys
for
Men and Boys

Volume II

By

Ray M. Russell and Ronny J. Coleman

Published By

Phenix Technology, Inc.
1504 Ave. de la Estrella, Suite F
San Clemente, Ca. 92672
(714) 498-1616

ISBN-0-910105-01-4

**Dedicated to collectors of Toy Fire Trucks
everywhere**

ABOUT THE AUTHORS:

Ronny J. Coleman

Ron originally started off to be a high school biology teacher. However he was side-tracked by a summer job as a firefighter with the U.S. Forest Service. He has since served in the U.S. Park Service, with the Costa Mesa Fire Department and finally as Fire Chief for the City of San Clemente, California. He has been Chief there since 1973.

Ron's interest in collecting fire service memorabilia was prompted by acquistion of a 1860's German fire helmet in 1964. He joined up with Ray's collecting in 1968 as a result of working together on the California Fire Show, sponsored by the Orange County's Fireman's Association.

Ron is the author of textbooks entitled "Management of Fire Service Operations" published by Duxbury Press, and "Fire Service Career Opportunities" published by National Textbook Company. He is also a consulting editor for Fire Chief Magazine and has written over 100 articles for magazines.

Raymond M. Russell

Ray started collecting toy fire trucks when his father, who was a San Diego firefighter, gave him an early Hubley ladder truck. At the age of seventeen, Ray became a firefighter himself. He has now served over 24 years in the fire profession. His experience ranges from the California Division of Forestry in Riverside County, Captain of Orange County Station 22, to his recent assignment in the field of Fire service training and education. For the State Fire Marshal's office in California.

Ray's collection, which started with his original Hubley fire truck in 1964, has never stopped growing. He still has the orginal Hubley given to him by his father. During his early years, his family moved several times. Ray recalls that on each occasion his parents would try to lighten the load by disposing of his toys. Ray would always recover the fire trucks and make sure they survived the move the next location. Today some of these toys have a great deal of value, both in monetary and nostalgic terms.

Both Ron and Ray are active in teaching Fire Service courses and developing curriculum. They have taught in many State and National Fire Academies, including there sponsoredby the International Society of Fire Service Instructors and The National Fire Protection Association.

ACKNOWLEDGEMENTS

As we noted in the preparation of Volume I, the task of putting a book together can verge on the monumental. It is a labor of love at time and at other times it can take on the proportions of the mythological cleaning of Greek Stables.

Ray and I would not have survived without the prodding and assistance of serveral friends and fellow collectors. We would like to thank the following people for their persistance and patience: Mr. Phil Glickman, Chuck Ford, Phil Prichard, Paul Talbott, Bob Guildig, Gerhardt Klarwasser, Chuck Satterfield, Max Schulman, Lisa Spinelli, M & K Printing, Murray Young and our two wives, Judy and Marie. If we forgot any one we apologize and will try to make it up in Volume III.

A1 TOY, made in Japan in 1960. This was a pressed tin toy. The serial number was D8133. The overall length of the toy was about 6½''. The toy was equipped with a friction drive and the siren operated when the toy was in operation.

ACCU-CAST, made in the United States, late 70's— early 1980's. The material is die cast. This model is a combination of a Mack Cab and an Ahrens Fox Front Mount Pump. Total length is 3 3/4''.

ACCU-CAST, made in the United States, era 1981. The material is die cast metal with rubber tires. It is a copy of a Seagraves Water Tower. The piece is very heavy. Total length is 4¼''.

ACCU-CAST, made in the United States in 1980. The material is die cast metal. This is an early version of a Ford Fire Apparatus. The total length is 2¾''.

ACCU-CAST, made in the United States in 1980. The material is die cast metal. This is a copy of an early Tootsie Toy. The length is 3''.

ACCU-CAST, made in 1979 in the United States. The material is very heavy meta, possibly lead. It is a copy of the Mack-''Bulldog.'' This company has reproduced many toys similar to the Tootsie Toy Company. It is 4½'' in length.

TO SPECIALIZE OR NOT TO SPECIALIZE

One of the first things that you will learn about when you start collecting Fire Truck Toys is that there are a million different types and kinds. Some are cheap . . . both in cost and construction quality . . . some are expensive and the possession of them borders on having the crown jewels.

This phenomena leads to one of the first dilemmas of the Fire Truck collector. Do you collect everything that comes off the manufacturers assembly line? What factors are involved in determining what you are going to try to collect?

Well, first off, you have to remember one thing about your collection: it's your collection and no one elses. A person who collects toy apparatus should not be influenced by the tastes of others, (that could be translated "prejudices") — you ought to collect what you want to collect. Generally, most people start off with very diverse tastes. They will pick up almost anything that remotely resembles a fire truck . . . it doesn't matter if it's a 10 cent piece of plastic or a real honest to goodness cast iron toy from the turn of the century. However, sooner or later you will come to the recognition that one of two things will come into play: Cost or Space.

Most of us simply cannot afford to have one of everything that has been produced. Don't feel bad if this realization has come to you. It has happened to us too. While we would like to own every toy in this book, the fact is that we don't. Many of them belong to friends who have been willing to share them with us. You should try to establish a budget for yourself when it comes to expanding your collection. There will be periods of time when you will not find anything new to add to the collection, but you should be putting away funds anyway. Next month, next week, maybe next year the opportunity will present itself and you will wish that you had the extra cash to pick up that "Find of a Lifetime". So . . . budget how much you can afford to spend on your collection and that may help you determine how much you can afford to be a specialist or a generalist collector.

The second aspect of a collection is the element of space. Notably, most really serious toy collectors homes look like a toy warehouse . . . every inch of wall space, shelf space, closet space and drawer space is full of the fruits of the collector's labors. This is not usually a real limitation to a collection, but it should be a consideration. Especially, if you are married and don't want to go to divorce court trying to explain to a judge why that wife of yours finally exploded . . .mine constantly is upset with the amount of dust that seems to accumulate around toys that are not under glass . . . so, what we are suggesting is that you budget your space too. Set aside an area that your collection will dominate and try to define your collection within that parameter.

Most collectors try to upgrade their collections by removing less desirable examples anyway, so by culling your collection and at the same time defining its limitations you can make a much better exhibit.

What are the different kinds of specializations that you can engage in? Well, how many differences are there? Some of the most obvious are collecting:

> A. From only one manufacturer
>
> B. Only one type of construction (slush cast, cast-iron,
>   die-cast, tin, etc.
>
> C. From only one country
>
> D. From only one era
>
> E. Only one type of apparatus

There are, of course, advantages and disadvantages of having a specialized collection. One can really fine tune a collection when they specialize. Costs may not be all that cheaper when you limit yourself to one area, because rarer pieces may be more and more difficult to obtain. Also, there may be periods of a real dry spell when your collection just doesn't seem to grow.

In all cases, the decision to specialize or collect everything that comes to your attention is a personal decision. If you can afford it, both financially and physically, the sky is the limit. If you have restrictions on either your funds or your domicile, then consider that specialization is not a disgrace. It is an opportunity to participate and contribute; an opportunity to become a real expert.

ACCU-CAST, made in the United States, manufactured 1980. The material is die cast metal with rubber tires. It is a copy of a Seagrave Pumper. Overall length 3½".

ACCU-CAST, made in the United States, late 70's—early 1980's. The material is die cast. It is a copy of a Mack Pumper. The total length is 3".

ARGO, made in the 1940's, probably the latter part of the decade. Manufactured in the United States. The material is tin. As the vehicle moves forward, the bell moves back and forth. This was part of a series of vehicles that included a taxicab, ambulance and others. Appears to copy the Hudson Hornet. Overall length is 4".

AUBURN, made in the U.S.A. in the late 1950's or early 1960's. Rubber-like material. No serial number. Length is 4¼''.

AUBURN, made in the United States in the early 1950's. The material is rubber. It is a copy of a transition piece from horsedrawn to motorized equipment. The overall length is 7½''.

AUBURN. Made in the U. S. A. in the mid 1950's. It is made of molded rubber. The serial number on the toy is 500. The overall length is about 7 3/8''.

AURORA PRODUCTS, made in the U.S.A. in the 1960's. A kit model. Completed length is 9½''. Patterned after the ALF Pumper.

AVIVA, made in Hong Kong in the 1970's. It is made of injection molded plastic. The serial number is 988RC. The overall length is about 10''. This is radio-controlled and has the cast of characters from "Peanuts" featured as the firefighters. The four characters are Snoopy, Woodstock, Linus and Lucy . . . Wonder why they never let Charlie Brown be a firefighter?

AVIVA, made in Hong Kong. The toy is die cast with some plastic parts. The serial number on the toy is C1. The overall dimensions are 2 9/16''.

AVON PRODUCTS, made in the U.S.A. in the mid 1960's, of glass. Length is about 6¼''. Contained after shave lotion.

BANDAI, made in Japan in 1980. The material is die cast metal with some plastic parts. It is a copy of a Chemical Fire truck used in Japan. The scale is 1/30th. The identification number is 12. The length is 3''.

BANNER TOYS, made in U.S.A. in 1952 of molded plastic. This toy has white body and red wheels. Also came as red body and white wheel. Could pass for an Alf Pumper. Length is 6¼''.

COLLECTION OR ACCUMULATION?

It's not very often that a person begins a "collection" by instantly obtaining the entire collection. No! If you are like most everyone else you probably got into collecting by starting off with a single piece, maybe a "set" of toys that someone gave you. In some cases the interest was self-generated by your own purchase of a toy. But, be honest! Did you really start off collecting fire toys or merely accumulating them?

Don't feel bad if that's the way you started. That's the way Ray and I got into the business too. In my case my wife gave me a toy fire truck for Christmas right after I was hired on the Fire Department. In Ray's case, his parents gave him a toy as a present one year. In both of our cases, the "collection" started with one!

But that's not the reason we put this material in the book. The number of pieces you have in your possession is really irrelevant. It's what you have done with the pieces that makes the difference between a collection and an accumulation. Maybe the two terms seem to be the same but they are not. Let me provide you with two definitions.

An accumulation is a gradual increase in the numbers of toys or other items that have come into a person's possession. An accumulation is characterized by being difficult to assess regarding the quantity, quality or desirability of the items being held. It is an amorphous entity, lacing structure and real value. Because, it it was stolen, damaged or otherwise disappeared the total loss would be difficult, if not impossible, to measure.

A collection, on the other hand, is a systematic identification, marking and displaying of toys or other items that are part of a larger body of collectibles. A collection is characterized by having a definite inventory, an estimated value, and an estimated value as well as an assessment of relative value of each of its components. It is a well-defined entity that has organization and a collective impact. If a collection is stolen, damaged or otherwise disappeared, the losses would be devastating to the owner, but measurable in terms of dollars and cents or intrinsic value.

Confused? Well, what we are saying here is that a collection of toy fire apparatus is not really a collection unless it has been identified, documented and properly stored or displayed.

Frankly, that's how Ray and I got into publishing this catalogue. We were trying to identify our accumulations . . . That's one of the reasons we have continued to document everything we can on toy fire trucks. Hopefully, those of you that are reading this, and Volume 1 are using the information to help you identify your toys . . . . . to put them into a context of some sort.

The index pages put into the rear of both volumes is designed to help you accomplish this task. We would like to encourage all of you to set down as you work your way through the catalogue and mark off the ones you have.This helps your collection in two ways . . . It lets you know what you really have and what you need to be looking for.

The second step to the establishment of a collection is to inventory your toys by assigning a number and approximate value to each piece. This can often be accomplished by attaching small "labels" to the bottom side of the toy. Each toy should have a specific number that can be cross referenced to an index card that contains the complete information on the toy. It's a good idea to even include the cost you paid for the toy when it came into your possession. As you find out information on the specific toy, you can add that information to the card.

In our case we have built a computer file that tracks our collection, including the photos we have taken of other people's collections.

When it comes to displaying a collection, the matter of space and taste must be addressed. In a lot of cases, the question of matrimonial stability may also have to be considered. Fire Truck collections have the tendency to become a major contender for space in the home. Therefore the real issue with displaying a collection is how to find a place that does not compete with the rest of the family and is relatively safe from two of the toy collector's worst enemies: small children and dust.

One of the simplest techniques is to get a glass fronted book case. This can get expensive and does have the limitation that they are often deeper than they should be to show off the toys. A simple, but unfortunately customized solution, is to fabricate a shelf-case that has the right depth and shelf height to show off the toys. In general this dimension means that the case should be no more than 3 inches for small scale toys and 6 inches for larger scale. The height of the shelves in the tiers should be no more than one and one half times the average length of the toys. Some collectors choose to place a small strip of mirror on the bottom of each shelf to give the collection a unique perspective.

If you are like the average Fire Truck collector, your acquisitions usually exceed the current planned-for space and the new offerings usually get set aside for a period of time before they are put into a proper place. But, don't let that set you back. Be disciplined as you acquire new additions to your inventory. Remember, it's not a collection until it has been: IDENTIFIED, DOCUMENTED, and PROPERLY DISPLAYED.

BK TOYS, made in Greece in 1965. The toy is
injection molded plastic. There are no serial numbers on the toy. The overall length is about 9''.
The toy is a wind-up type.

BRUMM, made in 1981, Italy. The material
is die cast metal. It is a copy of a Fiat 1100
Fire Chief's car from the 1930's. The toy is a
1/43 scale. Overall length is about 4''.

BREKINA, made in West Germany in 1983
of molded plastic. Length is 1½''. The roof is
removeable from this Volkswagon Jeep.

BREKINA, made in West Germany in 1982.
Made of molded plastic. 1¾″ long. Patterned
after the Opel P4 German Staff Car.

BREKINA, made in 1983 of injection molded
plastic. Made in West Germany. The model number
is DKW-F7. This toy was also used for advertising.

BREKINA, made in West Germany in 1981
of molded plastic. Measures 2″ and Fashioned
after the DKW F7 German Fire Staff Car.

BRITAIN LIMITED, made in England between 1948 and 1950. These crash firefighters came eight to a set. The overall height of the cast lead figures was about 54mm or 2 1/8''.

BUDDY ''L'' TRUCK, made in the U.S.A. of pressed steel with plastic parts. Made in the early 1980's. The toy was called the ''Brute'' Pumper. The catalog number on the package was 4945. The overall length was 5¼''. Original price, $3.79.

BULL CORP made in West Germany in 1977. Approximate length 9". Made of pressed steel, does have
some plastic. Serial number Bull 112. Features a
ladder that raises and lowers and rotates by hand.

BURAGO, made in Italy of diecast metal in 1982.
Some plastic parts. Serial number is 0179. Based
on the Lamborghini Cheetah. The front wheels
turn with the steering wheel. Length is 7¼".

CAPTINS, made of pressed tin in England in the
1980's. Used as a party favor to hold candy and
other items. Height about 4".

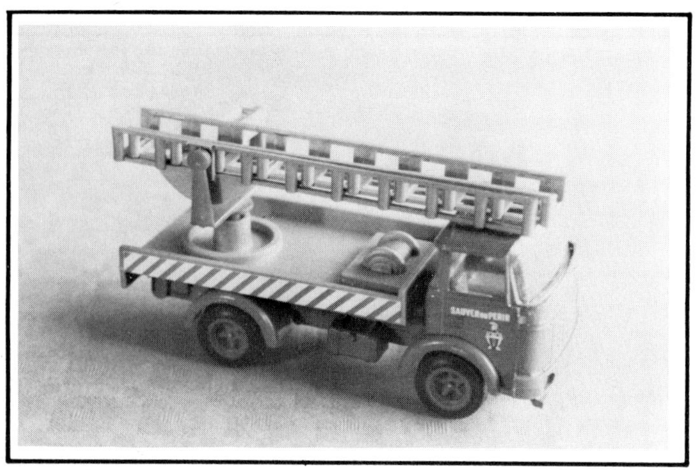

CHAMPION, made in about 1975 in France. The material is a die cast metal. This is a copy of a Berliet Apparatus. The ladder is made of plastic. Overall length is 4''.

CHICO TOYS, made in Columbia in 1975. Die cast cab and chassis with injection molded body and ladder. Serial number 20. Looks like a Mercedes Benz Latter Truck used in South America. Overall length is 6½''.

CLOVER TOYS, made of pressed steel. No information on country of manufacture. Made in 1983. Overall length is about 12''. Patterned after a Snorkel Fire Truck.

CONFRIEDES, made in France in 1983 of die cast metal. The serial identification is "CEF". This 10¼" long toy is based on a S2000 crash fire rescue vehicle. The compartment doors open.

CONRAD, made in Germany in 1980. It is of die cast metal with some plastic parts. It is a copy of a Rosenbauer Mercedes Benz Heavy Rescue truck. This truck is used a great deal in Austria and Germany. The truck is equipped to remove the box on the top with the small crane. Total length is 6".

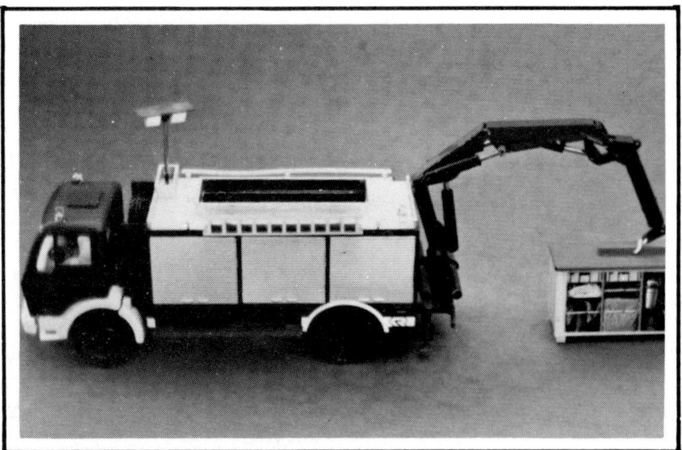

CONRAD, made in West Germany in 1982. The toys are die cast metal with a serial number of 3090. Based on the Mercedes Rosenbauer RFC-11 Rescue Truck. This shot shows the crane in action removing extra equipment. The overall length is 5¼".

CONRAD, made in West Germany in 1982 of die cast metal. Serial number is 5501. Based on the Rosenbauer Crash Fire Rig. Length is 7½″.

CONRAD, made in West Germany in 1981. The
material is die cast metal with some plastic parts.
It is a copy of a Rosenbauer Water Tender. Very
fine detail piece. The total length is 5''.

CONRAD, made in West Germany in 1982. The toy
is die cast metal with some plastic parts. There is a
serial number of 3490 on the piece. The overall length
is about 6¼''. It is patterned after the Rosenbauer
Rescue vehicle. It is a very finely detailed toy.

CONRAD, made in West Germany of die cast
metal in 1983. Has serial number of 5502.
According to our information this Pumper
which was called the Emergency 1 Pumper
was withdrawn after only 800 were made. The
truck is about 8½'' in length.

CONRAD, made in West Germany of die cast
metal in 1982. Serial number is 1017. Based
on the 1914 American LaFrance (Alf). Length 5 3/4''.

CONRAD, made in 1980 in Germany. The
material is die cast. The unit is a copy of a
Volkswagen ''Transporter'' Apparatus. The
model number is 3066. This is a 1/43 scale
model. Overall length is 4''.

CORGI, made in England in 1981. The material is
die cast metal with some plastic parts. It is a copy
of the HCB-ANGUS Firestreak Rescue Truck. It
has a removable chemical extinguisher on the side
of the truck, removable ladders on the roof and
a two tone horn. The lights flash off and on. It
two rescue crashmen. The total length is 6½''.

CORGI, made in England of die cast metal with a yellow plastic deck gun. This truck is based on the Chubb Fire Tender, made in the 1980's. The overall length is about 1 7/8''.

CORGI, made in England in the 1960's. Die cast metal with no serial number. It is paterned after the Chevrolet Impala of that era. Overall length is 4''.

CORGI, made in England in 1975. The material is die cast metal. This happens to be from the Turbine Truck series. It is 5½.. long.

CORGI, made in England in 1978 of die cast metal with a plastic ladder. This is the same toy as shown in Volume one except the shot is more detailed. There was a listed patent number on the bottom of 1278081. This could help in identification in future years.

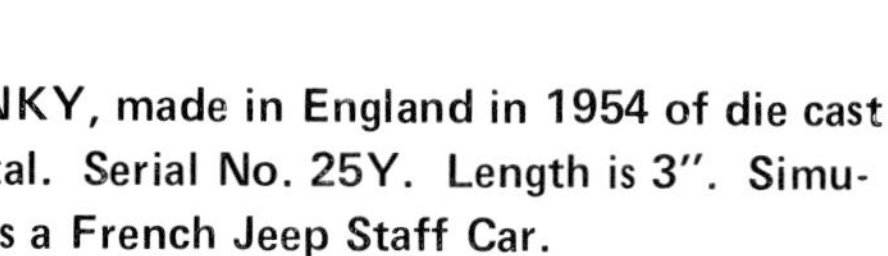

DINKY, made in England in 1954 of die cast metal. Serial No. 25Y. Length is 3". Simulates a French Jeep Staff Car.

DINKY, made in France of diecast metal about 1960. There is a serial number of 570 on the toy. Represents a French Rescue Van on a Peugot J7 chassis. All of the doors open. Length is 4".

DINKY, made in England in late 70's. Serial number 267. Made of diecast metal. Approximately 4.5'' long. The toy resembles the Squad 51 Los Angeles Fire Dept. Comes with two firemen and extra air bottles. It is one of the last few fire apparatus Dinky made.

DINKY. This toy was made in England in the early 1950's. It is made of injection molded plastic and was then hand painted. The toys are manufactured in the 1/48th scale. This set of 6 firefighters is based on a team of British firefighters.

DINKY, era 1978 made in England. The material is die cast metal with some plastic parts. The color is yellow. This unit was made for a very short time just before Dinky stopped production. It's a copy of an ERF Fire Tender. The overall length is 7''.

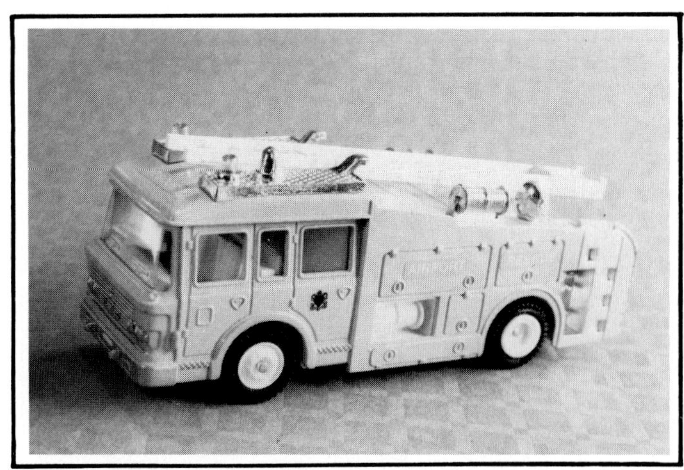

DOEPKE, made in 1952. Made of 18 guage steel. Earlier in 1950, Doepke buildt a 1/16th scale pumper patterned after the American LaFrance 700 Series. It had solid rubber tires and a baked enamel finish. In 1952, this version of the truck cam out with a searchlight attached.

DIFFERENT ANGLE of the same Doepke Truck. This truck came painted white and had a battery operation for the light. This version was different than the pumper that was built in 1952 in that it did not have the hose reel, a ladder or the hard suction hose. In 1952 these pieces could be purchased for around $16.00. Today they are probably worth between $250.00 and $300.00 depending upon their condition.

DURHAM INDUSTRIES, made in Hong Kong in 1977. The toy was made of injection molded plastic. It has a serial number of 5777. The overall length is 7¾". The motor was a wind-up type. This was a typical toy produced for the Walt Disney Productions of the era.

IT'S IN THE BOX!

What is the very first thing that most people do when they get home from the store with a new possession? Right! They rip open the sack, remove the new addition to their personal inventory and unceremoniously destroy the packaging that surrounds the object.

Does that sound familiar? Have you done it yourself? I'll bet that you have and I'll also bet that you will do it again. That is all the more reason why you should read this section. For it is that basic tendency that adds an interesting nuance to the Toys Collectors search.

One of the most difficult and often the most prized of finds is an old, rare or unique toy that is still in its original box! It occurs rather infrequently. The older and rarer the toy is the more the original container becomes a valued part of the toy. It's certainly no big deal to get the latest toys, like a Matchbox, in its original container. Everyone has one of those.

What we are referring to here is the fact that while toys have longevity, their packaging normally doesn't. To find a toy that is farily old, or fairly rare, especially one that has seen some actual use and yet have the box intact is a real addition to a collection. Generally speaking this phenomena is not all that unusual until the toy is at least 10 years old, preferably 20. There are some exceptions, such toys are limited editions.

There are several reasons why the box can add value to your toys. First off, by having the box you have a great deal more information about the toy itself. Printed on the original box is information regarding the manufacturer, materials of construction, date and numbers of issue. Sometimes the picture on the box will provide clues to all of the accessories that should accompany the toy. As most of you know, accessories are usually the first thing to go on a toy. The box illustration can often be a clue to the original decal placement, colors, etc.

Secondly, the presence of the box lends credibility to the fact that the toy is an "Original". Frankly, reproductions or copies of toys that are hard to distinguish from the original abound. But, the boxes of the originals are few and far between. It's far more difficult to create a counterfeit box than it is a casting.   The aging, the wear and tear on the cardboard and printed surface is extremely difficult to reproduce.

Thirdly, the existence of the original box gives a toy a sense of personality. If you have ever found a toy that has been obviously used, played with, perhaps even damaged and yet was somehow preserved in its original box, you know what I mean. It's a survivor and it's different Perhaps it had been stored for decades in an attic or garage. You often find yourself looking at that kind of toy in a different light; reliving the joys and fantasies of a child that first opened it up.   Perhaps that person is an adult now. Perhaps they are not even alive anymore. Why did they treasure that toy among others? Why was it so lovingly preserved? How many times did that toy almost get a trip to the dump or the Goodwill?

A toy in its original box has a character and a mystique all of its own. Often this factor can add a whole order of magnitude to the value of the toy. Interestingly enough the cheaper the original toy was, the more difficult it is to find one in the box. Expensive toys tend to have more rigid, better built containers. They tend to hold up better.

The more modern toys are going to be very difficult to assess in this light someday. Most of the modern packaging techniques almost require the total destruction of the containers to get the toy out. "Blister" Paks and cellophane windows might be cheaper to produce, but they are vulnerable. They tend to disintegrate with age. As a matter of practice, I try to keep from destroying the packaging of each new toy I add to my collection. (This has resulted in another problem. I now have a drawer full of invicerated boxes that appear to be well on their way to become a serious fire hazard.)

Lastly, the thing about toys in boxes is that they are easier to store, keep dust free and to retrieve. Not as much fun to exhibit, mind you, but efficient. Some collectors we have visited keep all their toys in boxes to keep them protected. This is especially true of the larger toys like "Buddy L" and "Tonka" or "Structo".

In reality, very few toys that are ever sold across the counter are ever kept in boxes. Every Christmas morning there are millions of toys opened. Their housings are tossed out, with no remorse, into fireplaces, crushed in trash compactors, or tossed in the trash. A fraction, a mere percentage of a percentage of them will ever survive their original owners.

Those toys that do make it, deserve a special recognition and place of honor in your collection. In our disposable society they represent a form of conservation deserving of toys that represent an occupation dedicated to the saving of lives and property.

EFSI, made in Holland in 1981. The material is
die cast metal with some plastic parts. It is a copy
of a Mercedes Benz Tanker. The words Brandwehr
means fire department in the Dutch language. This
particular toy has the telephone number for emergencies
on the vehicle. This number is common in Europe.
This concept is similar to the 911 system in this
country or the 999 in England.

EFSI, made in Holland about 1978. It is a copy of a
Mercedes Benz Aerial Ladder. The material is die cast
metal with a plastic ladder. This model also comes in
OD Green with military markings on it. The overall
length is 3''.

EFSI, made in Holland of die cast metal. No serial
number. This is a Mercedes Ladder Truck. Length 3''.

EFSI, made in Holland in 1981. The material is die cast metal with some plastic parts. It is a companion piece to the other toy shown on this page. It is a Heavy Rescue Wrecker Type vehicle. The words Brandwehr appear again. The color of the paint on this piece is referred to as "Day-Glow" red. Overall length is 3".

EKO, made in Spain in 1983 of molded plastic. 4¾" long. Designed after 1953-54 Ford Spanish Ladder Truck.

EKO, made in Spain in 1983 of molded plastic. Length is 1¾". Patterned after a Citroen French fire vehicle.

EKO, made in Spain in 1983 of molded plastic. Fashioned after a French Staff car. It measures 1¾''.

ELDON, made in the U.S.A. in the 1960's. Polyethylene plastic, 15½'' in length. Patterned after the Seagrave Pumper of that era. This toy had a companion piece that was an Aerial Ladder. The toy was red with gray trim. It pumps water.

ELIGOR, made in France in 1983 of die cast metal. The serial number is 1082. The chassis is a Ford. Length is 5''.

ELIGOR, made in 1981 in France. The material is die cast metal with plastic parts. It is a copy of a 1927 Renault Fire Apparaturs. Scale is 1/43. Overall length is 3½'. The unit also comes with extra decals.

FISHER PRICE TOY, made of pressed tin and plastic parts. The model was numbered 319. Made in the U.S.A. in the 1980's. Overall length about 15 inches.

FISHER PRICE, made in the U.S.A. in the early 1950's. It is made of wood and is about 12" long. This is a "Pull" type toy. When the toy was pulled across the floor the fireman bounced up and down and the bell rang.

FISHER PRICE, made in the U.S.A. in the early 1960's. It is made from wood and pressed cardboard. There is no serial number on the toy. Like all other pull toys this one was designed to ring the bell as the toy was pulled across the floor.

FJ TOY, made in France in the late 1970's. It is made of die cast metal with rubber tires. The material used on the roof is green plastic. It is a copy of a radio vehicle used by the French fire departments. It is 3" long.

FLEETWOOD, made in Hong Kong in 1975. This is injection molded plastic. This toy set was done after the popular show "Emergency" made the Squad 51 so popular. One thing to also note about collecting toys is that the modern packaging technique of "Blister Paks" can trap heat if the toy is allowed to sit in the sun. Too much exposure can ruin a toy. This toy is about 3" long.

FREEPORT TOY AND MANUFACTURING CO., made in the U.S.A. in the 1950's. Die cast aluminum. The serial number is 501. Overall length is 10''. This toy was shown in Volume one as a Manufacturer Unknown. Look on page 88. We were really off on the age in the first assessment.

MIGHTY MOVER, made in early 1980's. According to the package this toy was a "Fun Ho" toy that was diecast by Underwood Engineering Company Ltd. of New Zealand. The overall length is 2¼''.

FUNHO, made in Australia in 1978. The material is die cast aluminum. The toy is a reproduction of an early Arcade Pumper. The overall length is about 9½'' long. It has a model number of 105.

G.K. TOY CO., made in Japan in 1982. Made of molded plastic. 2½'' long. Serial No. MR10. This toy turns into a robot.

GAMA, made in West Germany in 1983. The toy is die cast metal. The serial number is 1606. It is patterned after a Mercedes Benz light wagon. The light mast extends. The overall length is 5''.

GAMA, made in West Germany in 1979. Serial number 2658. Made of injection molded plastic. Approximately 14″ long. The counterpart of this toy is Magirus German Aerial Ladder Truck. It features a water tank hose and small finger operated pump.

GAMA, made in West Germany in 1980. Injection molded plastic and the cab is of pressed steel. Serial number 434. Approximate length 10.5″. It uniquely features a water tank with pump and the ladder extends and raises.

GAMA, made in West Germany in 1979. The material is a combination of plastic and metal. This particular light wagon carried a battery and shed light over an area. The overall length is 7″.

GAMA, made in West Germany, manufactured about 1979. It is a copy of a Mercedes Benz Aerial Ladder. This latter is also seen in Book 1. In Book 1 however, the ladder was made of plastic. In this version the ladder is made of metal. Overall length is 5½''.

GAMA, made in 1980 in West Germany. The toy is die cast metal with plastic parts. It is based on the Krupp Chassissed Rescue Vehicle. The serial number is 9402. The scale is 1/32. The doors on the side and rear open. There is a shovel, pick-axe and a ladder on the top. Overall length is 6''.

GAMA, made in West Germany . The piece is die cast metal with some plastic parts. The serial number is 9123. The overall length is about 5¼'' long. It is patterned after the Faun TK Ladder Wagen.

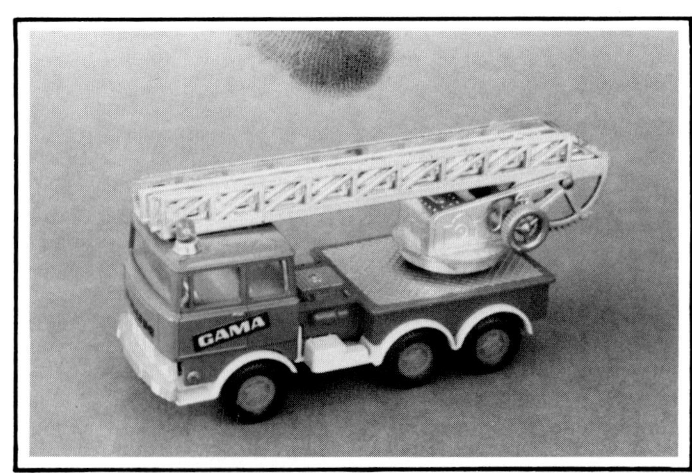

WHEN IS A TOY NOT A TOY?

That is the question! When does a toy fire truck stop being a toy fire truck and start being something else; a Collectible. The answer: Whenever the toy has a predefined scale and documented accuracy.

Hundreds of thousands of parents buy toy fire trucks for their children every year. At almost every Variety store, and at special toy stores, such as "Toys-R-Us", and FAO Schwarz there are racks and racks of toys to be picked over. Invariably, there are fire apparatus on these shelves. Fathers, Mothers, aunts and uncles often find themselves wandering the aisles looking for a toy for birthdays, Christmas stockings or special events.

Little do they realize that the "Toys" they select for gifts are no more intended to be played with than their real counterparts.

What we are referring to is the "Scale" model fire truck. First off, let's define some terms. Just what is a "Toy Fire Truck"?

A toy fire truck is an assemblage of metal, plastic, rubber or wood that is primarily designed to be handled by a child for purposes of entertainment. Its entire reason for existing is to provide enjoyment for a child of specific age group. It is designed to be used, abused and in general thrashed about in the fantasy world of youth. While it may be called a "Fire Truck" and in some ways even look like one, a toy fire truck is not accurate in its representation of a real piece of fire equipment.

Classic examples of this type of toy might be found in the Fisher-Price toy category. These toys are fire apparatus in a conceptual sense, but it would tax the imagination of the professional firefighter to compare his equipment to the toy version. Many times the only thing that makes a toy a toy fire truck is the presence of the color red, a decal that says "Fire Department" (or the abbreviation FD) and in some cases, wooden ladders on the side.

A Scale Model is different. A Scale Model is an assemblage of metal, plastic, wood or rubber that is primarily designed to be an accurate representation of a real piece of fire equipment. It is designed to a specific ratio of 1" equaling a certain number of inches in the real counterpart. A Scale Model is primarily designed to be collected and displayed as opposed to being used as a plaything.

The scales that we find Scale Toys in are commonly found to be such proportions as 1/32, 1/48, 1/64th and such. Some of them are designed to fit a "Gauge" like model trains. There is an "O" gauge and a "N" gauge.

Often the Scale Model is issued as a part of a series. The classic examples of this type series are the Wiking, Eligor, Corgi and Matchbox series. These apparatus represented in these lines are usually taken from the real apparatus in service in the country of origin. Sometimes the line will reflect a series of evolutionary development for a specific type of equipment.

Notably, most of the true Scale model apparatus are European in origin. The emphasis that is most often found in the European series are based on a specific manufacturer such as Dennis, Carmichael, Magirus, Mercedes Benz, Etc.

Another distinctive feature of the Scale model is that they often come equipped with detachable accessories and personnel that are built to scale also. Hose reels, ladders, boats, lighting gear, etc. are often inventoried with these Scale models to complete the model's authenticity. Unfortunately, these are often the first things to become lost after they have been taken out of the package.

The manufacturers of Scale toys often go to great lengths to maintain authenticity in their Scale models. Often doors will open, equipment will operate, lights and auxiliary equipment is properly located. In aerial equipment the outriggers work, the ladders raise, rotate and extend like the real thing.

Considerable emphasis is placed on the avoidance of relationships that are in proportion, such as wheels, ladders and so forth. The Scale models are often designed right off the blueprints of the original. Sometimes the same Scale model equipment will be produced in several scales. Sometimes the same Scale model will be produced with several different color schemes to indicate several applications for the same vehicle. Photos accompanying this section of the book illustrate these points. (Photos 76 and 52)

What all of this means is this. A person purchasing a "Toy" Fire Truck for a gift may or may not even care about these distinctions. Sometimes Scale models are given to children to play with just like any other toy. They often suffer in the process because they are not designed for that kind of handling. You may find examples of this as your collection grows. On the other hand you may find toys that were designed for children to handle and use that have never been taken out of their original boxes.

Both of these phenomena have their place in the collection. As a collector it is up to you to distinguish how you will approach the acquisition of the two types of items yourself. Toys are made to be played with and suffer a commensurate fate. Scale models are meant to be displayed and treated with reverence and respect. As your collection grows the presence of items that fit into both categories gives your collection character and distinction too.

FIREFIGHTING IN THE MOVIES

If there is any structure that is common in most communities it is the firehouse. From New York to Los Angeles, from the metropolis to the village, the sound of the firetruck's siren and airhorn is a common phenomena in society.

It's no wonder then that the firetruck has made its presence known in the movies too. Practically from the first day that movies were produced the fire truck became a prop. . . . Fire has been used as a special effect in so many famous movies that it could probably receive an Oscar for the most appearances.

Some of the earliest examples were found in the Max Sennett one reelers. While the name of the film is not in our files, it can periodically be seen on the television. In the film there is a "Keystone Kops" chase that involves a tillered aerial ladder. The ladder keeps swinging back and forth across the paths of different people, threatening to decapitate them at a moments notice.

One of the most popular films ever produced, "Gone With the Wind" made a spectacular use of fire as a special effect. Those that have seen the film, or recall the plot will remember that fire was used as a weapon of war and used to destroy Atlanta. One cannot help but wonder how the Atlanta Fire Department fared at the time?

Blackhawk Films, for a short time period used to have a short film entitled "Fireman, Fireman, Save My Child". This film, which was also available on 8mm, starred Buddy Hackett and of all people Hugh O'Brian . . . Which was quite a different role from his starring role as Wyatt Earp. The plot in this film was a little thin, but the heros were firefighters . . .

In the early 1960's a show was produced for television that starred firefighters. It was called "Rescue Eight". The main star of the show was an actor who was to later star in the infamous television soap opera, "Dallas". His name was Jim Davis. After the short run of the Rescue Eight show his face became well known as a character actor in western films. It was rumored that Jim and his partner . . . (whose name escapes me) . . . both were graduates of the Los Angeles Recruit Academy. From conversations that the author has had with those who recall the show it was one of the most authentic shows that has ever been done on the fire service . . . probably because it was done before all of the special effects people took hold of the plots.

Fire apparatus also starred in the film "Its a Mad, Mad World . . . This film, which for the lack of a better term was befitting its title, was a hysterical romp starring almost all of the bid name comedians of the era . . . Jonathan Winters, George Burns, Sid Caesar, etc. The final scene in the film consisted of a small army of people trying to escape from a hotel on an aerial ladder. Besides stretching the imagination, the directors in this case stretched the aerial to its ultimate destruction. One of the final scenes in the film shows the heroine standing on a turntable that is turning into a spouting fountain of blown hydraulic lines and twisted metal.

Another film which highlighted an actual fire apparatus was called "Those Magnificent Men in Their Flying Machines." The photo accompanying this section was taken from that film. In that particular production the English type Engine company was sent careening around the countryside everytime a "flying machine" was about to crash. As you can tell from the helmets on the firefighters the era was early in the century.

Probably the most classic of the firefighter movies was the "Towering Inferno". This film starred the most macho of men, Steve McQueen. As a Battalion Chief he performed practically every function on the fireground except to man the coffee pot in the staging area . . . but was the movie effective. Actually, very little apparatus was seen in the film, but the crews were given ample opportunity to demonstrate the equipment that is used in the high rise fire. "Towering Inferno" highlighted one key factor about fires and firefighting that has seemingly plagued the fire service in all films. Authenticity and realism do not go hand in hand with movie making. In order to "glamorize" the plot, the directors feel compelled to create unrealistic situations that real firefighters recognize and resent right away . . . Funny thing though . . . The public doesn't know the difference. If they believe that policemen get into high speed chases every day . . .then I guess that they can believe that firefighters can get blown down halls and get up to re-enter the fight without a scrape too . . .

The second television show that highlighted firefighters was called "Emergency". This series, produced by Jack Webb, who is a stickler for detail, almost made the words "paramedic" and "Squad 52" household words. It's highly likely that anywho collects toys will have at least one or two toys patterned after equipment from this show.

In general, this show was given high ratings by the professional fire service. One of the reasons for the high quality was the fact that the Los Angeles County Fire Department had technical advisors involved in almost all of the story development. They were not successful in achieving total authenticity, but they sure got close. As a matter of fact, many of the actors in the different scenes were actually off duty L.A. County Firefighters.

There are probably a lot of times that you have seen fire trucks or firefighters on the screen. Sometimes the cinema treats the fire service like society in general, they are taken for granted. Nonetheless . . . when the director wants to create some fear in the audience, what does he give them? You're right! A Fire. Regardless of whether the fire truck or firefighter is shown as a hero or a clown . . . he is treated kindly, for even the most reluctant of directors will admit that the firefighter will be around far into the future to provide something for the viewers. If this is not so, then what about Fahrenheit 451, Ray Bradbury's futuristic film about society some time hence?

This is a model done from an early Renault kit. The overall model is about 5'' long and is designed to illustrate a French Hose Wagon and Crew from the 1920's.

GLICKMAN TOY. This toy was made in the U.S.A. in about 1980. The toy was handmade of wood and plastic and was about 10''. It is based on a Mack apparatus from about 1920 and represents a Chicago Fire Dept. Light Unit. This was a prototype and was never manufactured.

GLICKMAN TOY. This toy was made in the U.S.A. in 1980. It is handmade from plastic and wood. The overall length was 4''. It was a conversion from a Ziss ''O'' Gage Rail Car used by the Union Pacific. This type of equipment was used to put out fires along the railroad right of way.

GLICKMAN TOY , made in the U.S.A. in 1932. The material is plastic and wood. This toy was made by a sergeant in the Feuerschutpolizel (Fire Protection Police) of the World War II era in the German army. The toy is a 1/32 scale. It was built from a photo of a model in the Berlin Fire Department.

GUISVAL, made in Spain in 1979 of die cast metal. The cab is a Volvo. One interesting point in this toy is the fact that the Spanish firefighters on this toy are wearing the fire helmet that was designed by the two authors of this book, Ray Russell and Ron Coleman. The toy's length is 5''.

GUISVAL, made in Spain in 1983 of die cast metal. Measures 3¼″. Simulates a Renault Spanish Chiefs car.

GUISVAL, made in Spain in 1982 of die cast metal. No serial number. Length is 2 3/4″. Cab is a Volvo.

GUISVAL, made in Spain of die cast metal in 1982. No serial number. Cab is a Volvo. Some plastic parts. Length is 3″.

GUITOY, made in Spain in 1979 of die cast metal. The hose feeds out of the side of the toy that looks like an Italian Crash Fire Vehicle. Length is 2 3/4".

HELLER, made in France in 1983. This is a plastic kit. Designed to represent a 1930 Citroen Fire Engine. Length is 8".

HELLER, made in France in 1981. The material is plastic. This model is made from a kit of a Delihay Aerial Apparatus. The scale is 1/25th. It has added equipment that is stored in the vehicle. The overall length is 3".

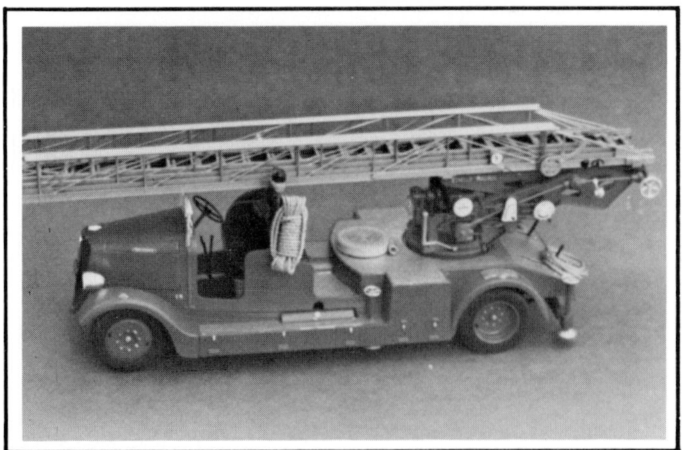

HELLER, made in France in 1983 of molded plastic. No serial number. This British Land Rover fire toy is 6" in length. This is a model kit.

HERPA, made in West Germany in 1980 of molded plastic. 2¼" long. Designed after the Volkswagon Fire Vehicle.

HERPA. This toy was made in West Germany about 1980. It is plastic injection molded. The serial number of the piece is 4053. The overall length is about 2". It is made in the Ho scale. Its real counterpart is a light rescue or staff vehicle.

HERPA, made in 1981, in West Germany. The material is plastic. The scale is about 1/87. The unit is a copy of a Ford Transist Fire Apparatus. The overall length is about 2''.

HERPA, made in West Germany in 1981. This toy is injection molded plastic. It has a serial number of 4034. The overall length of the toy is about 2''. This toy is modeled after the Volkswagen light rescue vehicle used in Germany. The color is "Day Glo" red, which was a popular fire apparatus color in Germany.

HERPA, made in West Germany in 1983 of molded plastic. Length is 2½''. Fashioned after a Mercedes Benz used as a Rescue or Utility van in the European Fire Series.

HERPA, made in West Germany in the early 1980's. It is plastic and was injection molded. The serial number on the toy is 4063. The overall length of the toy is about 1 7/8″ long. It was modeled after the "Range Rover" type vehicle that is used for rescue and staff and command functions. The vehicle was painted a very bright flourescent red.

HERPA, made in West Germany in 1982 of molded plastic. A Unimog pulling a rescue boat. The boat comes off the trailer. Length is 6″.

HERPA, made in West Germany in 1982 of molded plastic. Measures 2″. A replica of an Opel Ascona Chiefs vehicle used in Germany.

HERPA, made in West Germany in 1983 of injection molded plastic. No serial number. Patterned after the German Midmount Aerial Ladder on a Mercedes Benz chassis. The ladder extends to a height of 13½", has a basket for personnel. Length of toy is 4½".

GLICKMAN TOY.

HERPA. This toy was made in West Germany in 1982. It is injection molded plastic. There is no serial number on the piece. The overall length is about 2". The vehicle is based on a Ford Transit Utility Vehicle.

HERPA, made in West Germany in 1983 of molded plastic. No serial number. A Unimog Crew Hauler with a pump and hose trailer. Length is 3½".

HESS MFG., made in Hong Kong in the early 1970's. Injection molded plastic. This toy was made as a promotional for the Hess Oil Company on the East Coast. They were only available from that Company's Gas Station. Looks like a Mack Pumper. Overall length is 11".

HESS OIL COMPANY, made in Hong Kong in the early 1970's. It is injection molded of plastic. The overall length is about 12". It appears to be patterned after the American LaFrance Apparatus. It is battery powered and the lights on the top light up when the truck operates.

HIMALYA TOYS, INC. made in India in 1975.
Serial number 7. Approximately 8.5'' long.
Made of pressed tin. The motor is a clockwork.

HOT WHEELS, made in 1981 in the United States.
The material is die cast metal with some plastic
parts. The serial number is 1695. The vehicle is
called "Old Number 5". It is a copy of an Ahrens-
Fox Fire Apparatus. The overall length is 3¼''. One
of the nicer Hot Wheels models.

HOT WHEELS, another view of the Ahrens-Fox 5.
This toy has modified by adding the steering wheel
and tires off an IFSI Model T Ford. The toy was
also repainted, a gear shift lever was added. Tools
and equipment was added from other Ho scale toys.

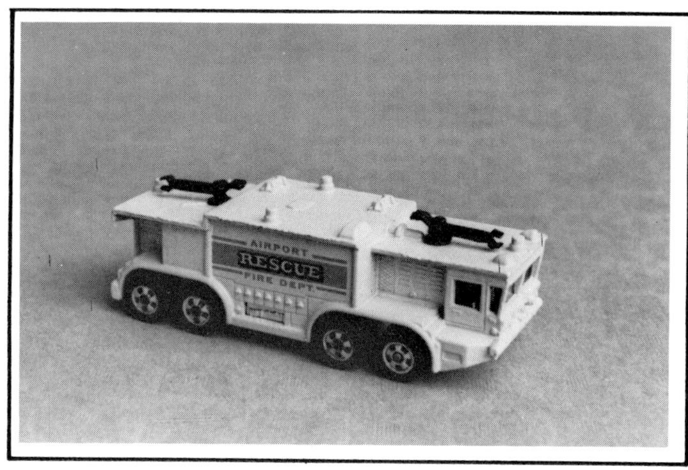

HOTWHEELS, made in Hong Kong in 1979 of die cast metal. Simulates Oshkosh Crash Fire Rescue Rig. The turrets are moveable. Overall length 3½''.

HUBLEY, made in the U.S.A. in 1952. This die cast model looks like an American LaFrance of that era. Suction hose and ladders removable. Length is 14''. This toy has been restored after being collected.

HUBLEY, made in the 1930's of cast iron with rubber tires. This toy was patterned after the Ahrens—Fox Apparatus that was very popular in that era. The overall length of the piece is 4½'', the width about 1 5/16''. The height of the top of the ball is about 2''.

HUBLEY (TINY TOYS) made in the U.S.A. in the 1960's. Plastic material, die cast base. Length is about 4 1/8''. Patterned after the ALF Pumper of that era. The two Pumper and the Aerial both came as either a completed toy or a kit. Original Pumper was a closed cab. The advertising for this toy was done by Art Linkletter of TV fame.

HUBLEY-GABERIAL, made in the U.S.A. in the 1970's. A white metal model kit based on the Ford Model-T, circa 1912-14.

HUBLEY, made in the U.S.A. in 1947 of metal. Approximately 10.25'' long. The toy is patterned after a 1947 Ford Service Ladder Truck. No serial number.

HUBLEY (Tiny Toys) Made in U.S.A. in the 1960's. Plastic material, die cast base. Length is about 6¾''. Fashioned after the Alf Aerial Ladder.

HUSKY, made in the U.S.A. Die cast metal, The toy was paterned after the Ford Thomas Van. The original came with a ladder on top. 1½'' long.

ZYLMEX, made in Hong Kong in the 1980's of die cast metal. The serial number on the bottom is P346. Overall length is 2½''.

INTERCARS. This toy was made in Spain in the early 1960's. The piece is made of die cast metal. The serial number is 2026 and is manufactured in the 1/43 scale. It is patterned after a Spanish Staff Vehicle.

IRWIN, made in Fitchburg, Massachussetts in the early 1950's. Plastic materials. Serial number is 1301. The toy has some unique features. The headlights go up and down and the firefighter's head bobs up and down when the toy was pulled. The length is 13''.

JIMSON TOY, made in Hong Kong of injection molded plastic. The toy has a wind-up motor on the left side. The overall length is 3''.

JIMSON, made in Hong Kong of injection molded plastic, made in the 1980's. The serial number is 253. The original cost was $1.49. Overall length is 2½''.

KIT-JOHAN, made in U.S.A. in 1976 of molded plastic. 7¼'' long. Patterned after a 1928 Mack Aerial Ladder. Made by Phil Glickman.

MFG. UNKNOWN, maybe Johillco, but cannot substantiate that. Made in England in the early 1940's of cast lead. The arms on these toy firefighters swivel. The overall height is about 4''.

These two trucks are in the "Special Library Collection" in the San Francisco Library. Neither of them have names of manufacturers on them. The tin truck has the letters OROBR on it. It is possibly from Germany. They are cast iron on the Steamer and the Crew Truck is pressed tin. They are both about 5½" long.

KAY TOY, made in approximately 1952 in Japan. The material is pressed tin. The serial or ID number is 110. It is a copy of Hudson Hornet Chief's car. It is one of the collector's items that has become very popular with tin toy collectors. They are hard to find in this size. Overall length is 4".

FIRE DEPARTMENT

CITY OF LOS ANGELES, STATE OF CALIFORNIA

To all to whom these presents shall come, Greeting:

This is to Certify that under the provisions of the Charter and Ordinances of the City of Los Angeles, J. H. Anderson was appointed a member of the Fire Department of said City with rank as Fireman on the 14 day of Feb. '12.

PROMOTED TO REGULAR

AUTO FIREMAN _______________________   ASSISTANT CHIEF _______________________

ENGINEER _______________________

LIEUTENANT April 20, 1922.

CAPTAIN _______________________

BATTALION CHIEF _______________________

RETIRED ON PENSION ROLL

ATTEST:

Board of Fire Commissioners

BY _______________________ SECRETARY.

_______________________ CHIEF ENGINEER.

NOTE: This Certificate valid only when properly filled out and signed by Secretary, and dates other than original appointment attested by signature or initials of Sec'y.

KEITH SMYKAL CO., made in U.S.A. in 1975. Serial number 11. Made of blown plastic. Approximately 11.75" long. The toy resembles a Mack Pumper and is used as a bank.

KEYSTONE, made in U.S.A. in 1946-50. Injection molded plastic. Length approximately 4". Unit on the right has small finger operated water pump. No serial number.

KEYSTONE, made in the U.S.A. in the early 1950's. It is made of fiberboard and wood. The toy is about 12" square. It is patterned after an old Fire Station. The Station had a bell and the doors wind up.

KEYSTONE, made in the U.S.A. in the mid 1950's of wood and pressed board. The doors were metal. The crank on the side of the toys would pull the doors up. The vehicles were pushed out by a spring. 17" long by 9" in height.

"BASHING" A KIT OR TOY

One of the things that happens to most Toy Collectors sooner or later is that they succumb to the temptation to modify a toy or scale model. There are lots of different opinions on this practice. Some people believe that to convert or modify any collectible is a violation of the principle of having a "pure" collection. Others believe if you cannot find a toy or scale counterpart of a piece of equipment you want in your collection, then it's OK to modify a piece to achieve your objective.

In either case the question of "Bashing" or modifying a kit is important to a collector. First off you need to know that it's done and that you may find a piece that just doesn't seem to appear in any catalogue. Look for the clues that a piece has been modified if that happens. Some of the most telling clues are the presence of a basic chassis that is identifiable. The second clue is to look carefully at the means and methods used to attach accessories to the item. Bashing often results in a poor match in this area. Of course, some of those that are really good at this technique will disagree on this point!

The following photos are of models done by Ray Russell for his personal collection.

KITBASH, made in the U.S.A. from molded plastic. This model was to simulate a WW II BMW military fire motorcycle. The German army used these in their campaigns. The pump was operated by the motorcycle motor. The model is about 11″ long.

This model is also based on the Revell ZIS-6 kit. It is a Russian Pumper from the same era as the Aerial Ladder. It uses both Revell parts and scratch-built parts. The overall length is about 6″.

KIT BASH, made in the U.S.A. from molded plastic. This is a Van Pelt Engine Company on a Kenworth chassis. The cab is 1/32nd scale. The rest of the body and the tires are 1/25th.

KIT BASH from A. Brumm. Length is 3 3/4".
An Italian staff car.

KIT BASH from an Eligor. This French die
cast is about 4¼" long and is based on a 1930's
Ford chassis.

KIT BASH from an Eligor. This die cast toy was
converted to look like a 1939 Mercedes Wartime
Fire Engine. Length is 5".

KIT-BASH LINDBERG, made in England in
1976. Made of molded plastic. Serial No. 23.
Length is 4½″. Resembles a Holland or Denmark
GMC fire engine, made from an altered school
bus kit. Model by Ray Russell.

KIT BASH-OLD CARS. This toy which was
made in Italy in 1982 represents an Italian pumper.
The doors open. Length is 5″.

KIT-PRECISION MINIATURES, made in U.S.A.
in 1982. Made of die cast metal. Measures 6½″
long. Simulates a 1932 Duesenberg. The siren
and red light on the front bumper is black and
white.

KIT BASH from a Siku. The Siku had a serial number of 311-0215. This simulates a Hanomac Water Tanker. Length is 4".

KIT BASH from a Solido. Overall length is about 5". French type pumper on a Fiat chassis.

KIT BASH SOLIDO. This is a Citroen C4F Pumper and Hose Tender. Length is 4½".

KIT BASH SOLIDO. This French made toy was made in 1981. The material is die cast metal. The toy firefighters are Starlux. This represents a 1930 Citroen Crew Truck. Length is 4″.

KIT BASH from a Solido. This was made to look like a 1930 French Citroen C4F Hose and Crew Wagon. Length is 4.5″.

KIT BASH from a Solido Toy. This made form the station wagon with the serial number 66. Overall length is about 4″.

MODEL-BASH WIKING from West Germany, 1979. Made of molded plastic. Measures 3″. Serial number 3350. A copy of a Homemade Fire Truck by a German Volunteer Fire Dept. Model by Ray Russell.

KIT BASH. This is a Monogram kit that was converted to a Baltimore High Pressure Unit. The kit was plastic with some metal parts. No serial number. 1/24 scale about 10″ long. Made by Harry Davis of Laurel, Maryland by using the "Logger" truck chassis, A.I.M. nozzles and accessories.

LANTERN BRAND TOYS, made in Hong Kong in 1976. The toy is injection molded plastic. No serial number. The overall dimensions are 11″. The toy is battery operated and is called the "Bump and Go" type.

LANTERN TOYS, made in Hong Kong. This toy was injection molded from plastic. The serial number is 1081. The overall length is about 10″. It represents a Fireboat. But it is not patterned after any particular one. The toy was battery operated and would squirt water when it was moved across the floor.

MATCHBOX (Lesney) made in England in the 1970's. This was a Ford Tractor pulling a Dixson Low Boy Trailer. The truck and tractor were designated as K7. The dozer was K17. The overall length was 9″. The tractor was painted red, the low boy, green and the dozer red.

LINNEMAR TOYS, made in Japan in the early 1960's. The toy is pressed tin. The serial number is 10. The overall length is about 12½". It is possibly patterned after the American LaFrance Apparatus. It is battery powered.

LITTLE PEOPLE, made in Hong Kong in the 1970's. The material is injection molded plastic. The equipment had a cardboard "Firehouse" too. The Firehouse was open at the top and folded up for storage. Overall length is 4".

LJN TOYS, made in Hong Kong in 1980. This is a die cast metal toy with some plastic parts. It is patterned after a LA County FD Rescue Squad on a Chevrolet 1 ton chassis. The overall dimensions are 2¾".

LUCKY TOY, made in Hong Kong in 1978. The material is plastic. It is a copy of a Berlay Aerial Ladder from France. The markings are British. It has friction motor on the front wheels. The identification number is 3121. Its overall length is 7".

LUSO TOYS. Made in Portugal in 1979. They are made from die cast metal. The serial number is 11179. They are manufactured in the 1/43 scale and are about 7" long each. The vehicles represent a Citron GS 1220 Brea Pallas. Used as a rescue vehicle.

LYRA, made in Greece in the 1980's. The toy was plastic with a serial number of ML1200. The battery made the toy go forward, reverse, right and left. The overall length was 14".

MAJORETTE, made in France in 1981. It is a die cast metal toy with some plastic parts. It is patterned after a 4x4 Unimog Fire Apparatus used in Germany. The overall dimensions are 2 1/8''.

MAJORETTE made in the 1980's in France. Die cast metal with many plastic parts. The truck is entitled "Mercedes Pompier Aeroport." The model number is 258. Overall length is 3''.

MAJORETTE, made in France in 1980. The material is die cast metal with some plastic parts. The unit is a copy of a French "Gazelle" Helicopter. The scale is 1/70th. Its identification number is 371. The overall length is 5½''.

MAJORETTE, same helicopter except showing that the blades on the helicopter fold up.

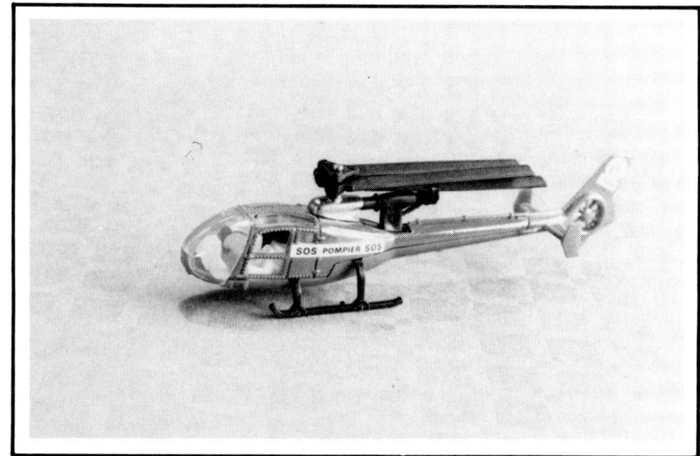

MARX, made in the United States in 1954. The material is plastic with hard rubber tires. It has a wind-up motor. When it operates it makes a siren noise. The overall length is 12''.

MATCHBOX (Lesney) made in England in 1978. Serial number K67. Approximate length 4.5''. It is made of de cast metal and comes in lime yellow and red. It resembles a Dodge Monaco Fire car.

MATCHBOX (LESNEY) made in England in 1981.
The toy is die cast metal. Toy designed to look
like a Crown Snorkel, but has a rear mounted pump.
This is another version of the Matchbox toy shown
in Volume one on page 77, middle picture. Length
is about 3".

MATCHBOX (LESNEY) made in England in 1981.
This is a die cast toy. Based on the Code Red Series
on TV. Styled after a Mercury Fire Chief's vehicle.
No serial number. Length is 3".

MATCHBOX (LESNEY) made in 1981 in England.
Part of the "Code Red" series. The model number
is 01-02-94. The overall length is 3". It is interesting
to note that this "Fireboat" comes equipped with
wheels. The original selling price of this toy was
$1.99.

MATCHBOX (LESNEY) made in 1981, made in England. It is a die cast metal toy patterned after a pumper shown on the "Code Red" Television series. The serial number is 01-02-95. The overall length is approximately 3". The pumper had Los Angeles City Fire Department on the door and P1 on the roof. This came as a part of a series of 8 different toys.

MAXWELL, made in the 1980's in Hong Kong. Made of die cast metal. The ladder is plastic and extends. It was interesting to note that several of these toys were shipped to the United States in a variety of colors. Some were green and blue. The tractor detaches from the trailer.

MAXWELL, made in India in 1980. The material is die cast metal. The serial number is 520. Based on the "Ambassador" Fire Service Staff Vehicle. Overall length is about 3½".

MAXWELL CO., made in India in 1978. Diecast metal. Serial number 514. Approximately 2.75" long. This toy is patterned after a Lincoln Continental. It features a green light on top of the roof.

MAXWELL/MILTON CORP., made in India in 1980. No serial number. Made of die cast metal. Approximately 4" long. Patterned after a Chevy Fire Chief's car. ('59 Chevy Impala)

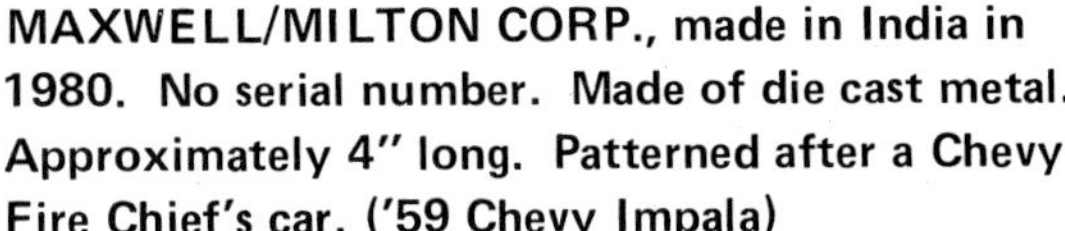

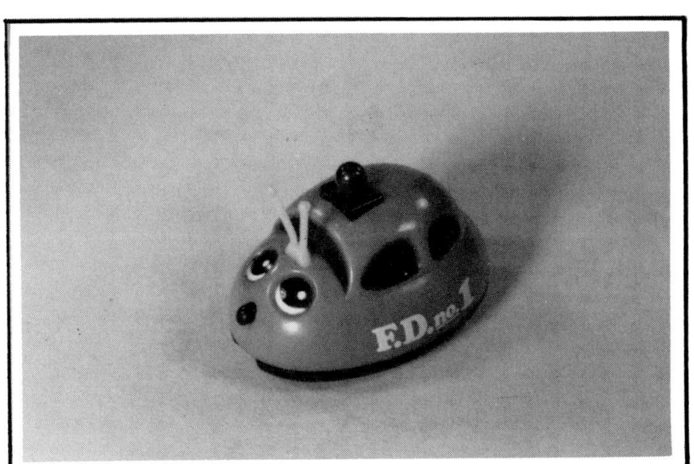

MEGO CORP., made in Hong Kong of injection molded plastic. This toy was called the "Doodlebug." Overall length is 2 3/8".

MERTEN, made in West Germany in 1976 of injection
molded plastic. Serial number is OXN-2377, Ho
scale. Ho German firefighters with ladders, nozzles,
hydrants, hoses and axes.

MFG. UNKNOWN. Made in Hong Kong in the
early 1970's. Note that this toy had a pump that
would squirt water through a plastic hose. The
firefighters are in British attire.

This is the rest of the "Wheaties" series that was shown in Book one on page 45. There were actually five in the set. They were made about 1954. The five pieces have the following serial numbers: the Chief's car, the number 6 on the underside. The Chief's car also has KFD impressed on the hood and trunk. The High Pumper has the serial number 18. The Pumper has the number 15. The lower Pumper has a number of 26. The Aerial Ladder is numbered 23.

MFG. UNKNOWN, made in the U.S.A. about 1980. This Christmas tree ornament is made of fire plaster. No serial number. Overall length is 2½".

AMERICAS 6 Frontpiece. This was the Fire Company that was run by the infamous "Boss Tweed" of Tammany Hall.

MIGNOT, made in France around 1979—80. It is made of pressed lead and die cast metal. There is no serial number on the toy. The overall length, including the horses is about 7½″. The horses are cast solid. The ladders are removable. It is patterned after a French Ladder vehicle of the late 1800's.

MIGNOT, made in France in the 1960's of die cast metal and hand painted. There is no serial number on the toy. It is made to the 1/32 scale and is about 3″ long. This piece depicts a messenger in the army fire service from the time period of about 1910.

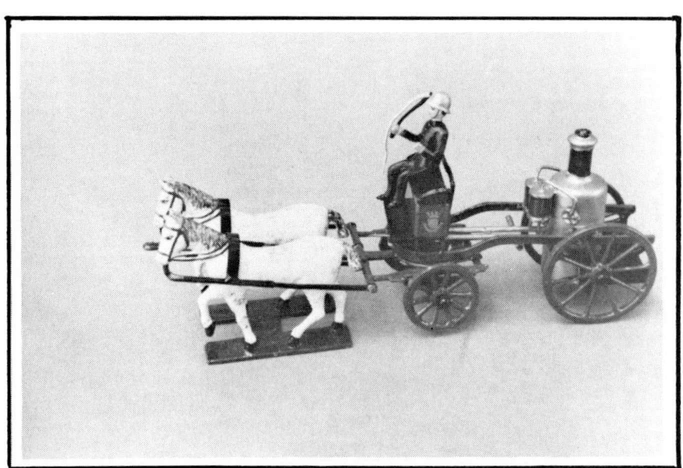

MIGNOT, made in France in 1980. This is a pressed lead and die cast metal toy. There is no serial number. The overall length is about 7½″. The piece is patterned after a French Steamer of the late 1800's.

MIGNOT, made in France in the early 1940's, of die cast metal. There are no serial numbers. The toys are done in the 1/32 scale. These toys also represent French "Soldier-Firefighters" of the French army. (Note the name Mignot is pronounced Meen-Yo).

MIGNOT. Made in France in the late 1970's. It is made of pressed lead and die cast metal. There is no serial number. The overall length of the toy is about 4¾". The toy was listed as a Fiat motor truck from the early 1900's. Only one driver came with the toy.

MIGNOT, manufactured in France in the early 1940's. This is a die cast toy. The toy is of the 1/32 scale. It is based on the "Soldier-Firefighter" from Napoleons army. The complete set consists of an officer and five enlisted men from the "Sapeurs-Pompiers".

MIGNOT, made in France in 1979. This is a cast lead toy that is hand painted. The height of the toy is about 2 1/8". The set of 12 firefighters is accompanied by the 9 soldiers on parade. This set reflects the French heritage of the firefighters being closely allied with the military. These are patterned after turn of the century firefighters.

MFG. UNKNOWN, possibly the same as the glass toy shown previously on this page. Made in the early 1940's. The material is glass with the same design as the 1914 version, only all parts are glass, including the wheels. Overall length is 4½".

MFG. UNKNOWN, made in Germany in 1968 of die cast metal. Models measure 2" each and represent a water tanker, hose crew, pumper, salvage crew, and ladder truck.

MINIMAC, made in Brazil in the 1980's. The material is die cast. It is a copy of Ford Jeep. The scale is 1/43. The length is 3''.

MIRA, made in Spain in the late 1970's. The material is die cast metal. The ladder is plastic. Overall length is 4''. Its scale is 1/64.

MIRA, made in Spain in about 1980. This is a die cast toy. The serial number is M4003. The toy is manufactured to the 1/43 scale and has an overall length of about 3½''. It is patterned after the VW Sirocco T. The piece was painted a dark maroon. The doors open.

This is a Clay Model of an Aerial Ladder being designed for the American LaFrance Fire Company. This particular model was built to scale for the use of the company in evaluating certain design features. It was about 3 feet long. What a prototype for a toy fire truck!

MIRA, made in 1975 in Spain. The material is die cast metal with a plastic aerial. The scale is 1/64. The word "Bombero" on the side stands for "Firefighter". It is approximately 8½" long.

MOCKBN, made in Russia in 1978. Serial number A5. Made of die cast metal. Approximately 4" long. The toy originally represented a Russian Service vehicle. It has since been converted into a fire toy. The hood opens to reveal a motor.

MFG. UNKNOWN. Made in Hong Kong in 1980. The material is die cast metal. The toy has a serial number of E-32. The overall length is about 4¾". It is patterned after the Aloutte III.

MFG. UNKNOWN, Era early 1940's in the United States. The material is cast aluminum. This is a typical example of toys that often have to be purchased without their parts. The overall length is 12".

RED CHINA TOY made in about 1975. This toy is made of pressed tin and some plastic. The serial number on the toy is MS090. Its overall length is about 6¾". It is patterned after the VW fire vehicle and has wind-up motor. It is rare to get toys out of Communist China at this time.

MR. TIDY TOY, made in the U.S.A. of molded rubber. This was a container for bath soap for kids. The container held 11 fluid ounces of soap. There apparently was a ladder on the top at one time. Unknown date of Manufacture.

This is a MOSIAC MURAL honoring an early Fire Chief in the City of Anaheim, California. Reportedly the chief's name was John Rimpau. The mural is located on a Savings and Loan Building at Harbor Blvd., just north of Disneyland.

MFG. UNKNOWN. Possibly an early Kingsbury. Made in the United States. Era about 1915. The truck is fabricated in pressed tin metal with wooden ladders. When the ladder is released it goes up under spring power. It has a wind-up spring mechanism to power the back wheel. The ladders of the truck are red—The body of the truck is blue and the wheels are gray. That does not look like the original steering wheel on the unit. Overall length is 9''.

NEW TOYS INC., made in India in 1977. Approximate length 4''. Made of pressed tin and some plastic. No serial number. Uniquely features TO friction drive. Cab has sparks flying around as toy rolls forward.

NOREV, made in France in 1982. The serial number is F-89. Based on a Volvo Crash truck. The overall length is 2¾''.

NOREV, made in France in 1980 of molded plastic. The serial number is 26. A Citroen van. Length is 3½''.

MFG. UNKNOWN, made in Japan of pressed tin. Probably made in the 1950's. Overall length is about 5''.

NYLINT TOY CORP., made in the U.S.A. in 1975. Pressed steel and injection molded plastic. Good heavy duty toy. Length is about 10''.

OLD CARS, made in Italy in 1983. No serial number. Approximately 4.25'' long. Made of die cast metal with a plastic tank. The toys resemble an Italian Fiat 90 Water Tender Fire Apparatus.

OLD CARS, made in Italy in 1982. Made of die cast metal. Approximately 5'' long (1/43 scale). It resembles a Fiat&Inveco Rescue Vehicle. All doors open. It is a finely detailed model. No serial number.

OLD CARS, made in Italy in 1979. This die cast
toy represents a Fiat Campagnola Fire Radio Unit
with a generator trailer. Length is 6'' with the
trailer.

OLD CARS, INC., made in Italy in 1980. Die
cast metal. Based on the Fiat-Iveco Fire Crew
Hauler. Length is 4¼''.

OLD CARS, made in Italy in 1983. No serial
number. Approximately 3.5'' long. Made of die
cast metal. It looks like a Fiat Campagnola Jeep
type of light unit. The hood opens and shows
motor inside.

MFG. UNKNOWN. Possibly made in Hong Kong. The unit is made from die cast metal. Fire Chief's car. Total overall length is 2¼''.

MFG. UNKNOWN, made in France in the early 1980's. The material is die cast metal. It appears to be a copy of an earlier FJ toy found in Volume one on Page It is approximately 4'' long.

ORIGINAL (JUNIOR) PRODUCTS, made in Japan in the late 1970's. It was made of pressed tin and some plastic parts. There was no serial number. The overall length is about 12½''. The toy was battery operated.

MFG. UNKNOWN, made about 1958 in Japan. The material is tin. The toy is a copy of a late 1950's GMC fire truck with a crew cab in the back. The overall length is 7½".

MFG. UNKNOWN, made in the U.S.A. in the 1950's. Molded rubber with no serial number. The overall length is 4".

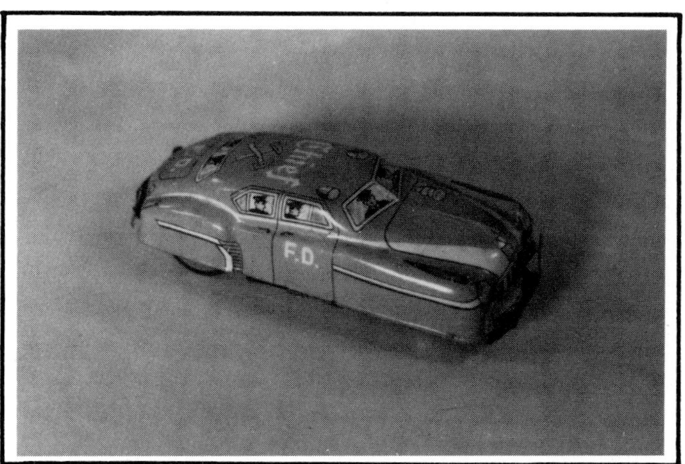

MFG. UNKNOWN, made in Japan in the 1950's. This toy may be a "K" Toy, but the lettering on this one is difficult to read. The license number on the toy was FD 110. Overall length is 3 3/8".

MFG. UNKNOWN, made in Hong Kong of in-jection molded plastic. The toy has a wind-up motor on the left side. The lettering on the truck and the detail is provided by a paper-like decal. Overall length is 3½''.

MFG. UNKNOWN, made in Mainline Chins in 1979. Serial number 409ME699. Approximately 10'' long. Made of pressed tin. Motor is battery driven. The pump panel lights up.

MFG. UNKNOWN, made in Communist China of pressed tin. This toy was brought back to the U.S.A. in 1983. Overall length is 3¾''.

COSTA MESA
CHAMBER
COMMERCE
GARAGE
CMFD

SEMPER VIGILANS
COSTA MESA FIRE DEPT
STATION NO 2
ENGINE CO. 2

"Pyro McPhobia"

a fear that a bunch of clowns might show up to put your house fire out.

"Any Fire Equipment desired on chassis you specify."

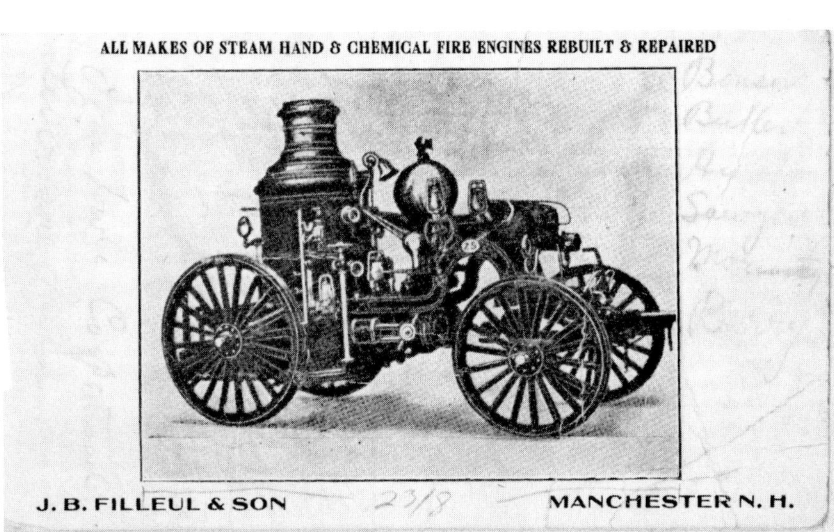

Ruins of the Great Chelsea Fire, Sunday, April 12, 1908.　　　　Lynn Fire Engine No. 1

Remember the film ''Towering Inferno''? Well, this is one of the helmets that was worn in that film. It had an interesting demise also. Ray had portions of the collection on display at the California Fire Marshal's office in Sacramento. Unfortunately, the building was burned to the ground as a result of an arson fire set next door. . . The helmet had its moment of glory on the screen and then went the way of a lot of real fire helmets . . . destroyed in service!

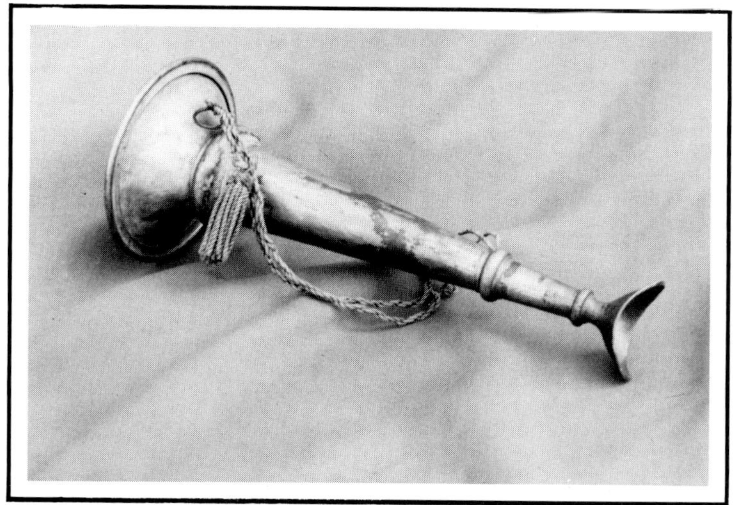

The Speaking ''Trumpet'' is the symbol of rank in the fire service. In the early days the Trumpet was used to amplify the voice of the foreman of the fire company. Often the Trumpet was very plain like this for fireground use. Another version that you can often find is more ornate and was given to Chiefs as a special gift upon retirement or a special occasion. If you look at a modern firefighter's badge you will find crossed trumpets that stand for the different ranks of the fire service. A lieutenant has one trumpet on a silver badge, a fire chief has five crossed trumpets on a gold badge.

The "Classic" Cairns style Fire Helmet. This helmet is from the San Francisco Fire Department and was in service until a very few years ago. The helmet is made of leather with a metal "Phenix" on the top.

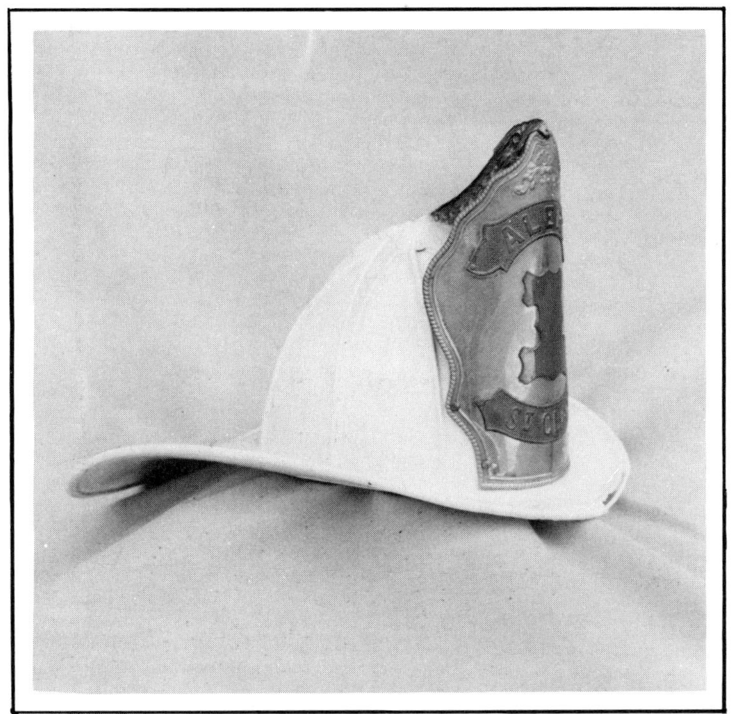

Early on the fire helmet was not just a means of personal protection. It was also a means of identifying status in the community. This helmet, manufactured by Cairns around the turn of the century or earlier was a "Parade" helmet. The frontpiece is silver and brass. The high peak, the fine stitching and overall appearance were designed to impress onlookers.

Another version of the "Parade" style Cairns helmet is this type. This helmet, from Eagle Hose is very light weight. It obviously had very little utility at the scene of an emergency. The fancy swirl to the "Combs" on the cranial portion of the helmet and the stylized top piece point to the use of this helmet to impress the civilians.

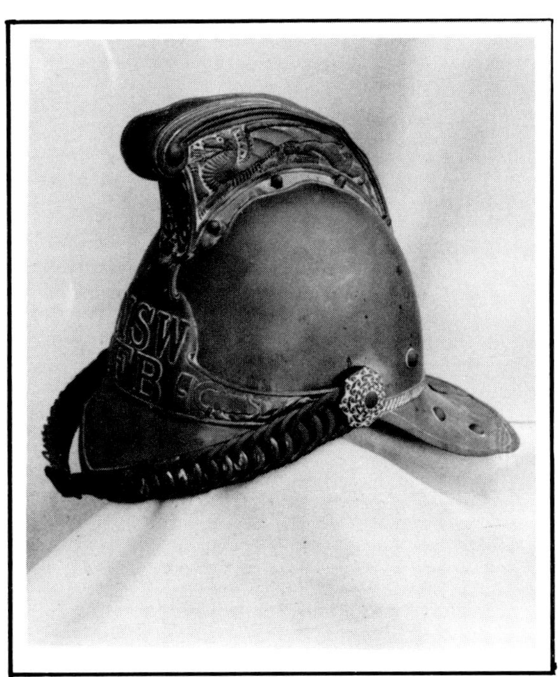

In the European context the fire service had a military background. You will note that many of the helmets from the continent look like the military helmets from the same era. This helmet is from New South Wales in New Zealand. Interestingly this helmet is made from brass and in World War II the Allies melted down a lot of brass fire helmets to make ammunition. This helmet, polished up and properly displayed is a real joy in a Fire collection.

This leather helmet is from the Liverpool Salvage Corps in Great Britain. That's what the LCS stands for on the front of the helmet. You will often see Fire Truck toys from the UK that are patterned after American fire apparatus that are wearing a helmet shaped somewhat like this profile. That's often a clue to where a toy was manufactured. While the toy designers can work off plans of the truck to design the casting they often look "out the window" as passing fire apparatus and pattern the firefighters after the ones they can relate with.

Greek firefighters respond to emergencies wearing a helmet that hasn't changed in profile for thousands of years. This shell is patterned after a military type helmet. Note the ornate decorations on the metal work.

YOSEMITE NATIONAL PARK
1-73174

In France the fire service is part of the military establishment. This all brass helmet represents the style that most of the departments in that country wear. The metal frontpiece is detachable from the helmet. That's very much like the leather frontpieces we use in the U.S. to designate the location from which the helmet comes.

A lot of people don't realize that the Vatican in Italy has its own Army, Police, and Fire Departments. This metal helmet is from the Vatican Fire Service. Note the cross on the Frontpiece of the Helmet!

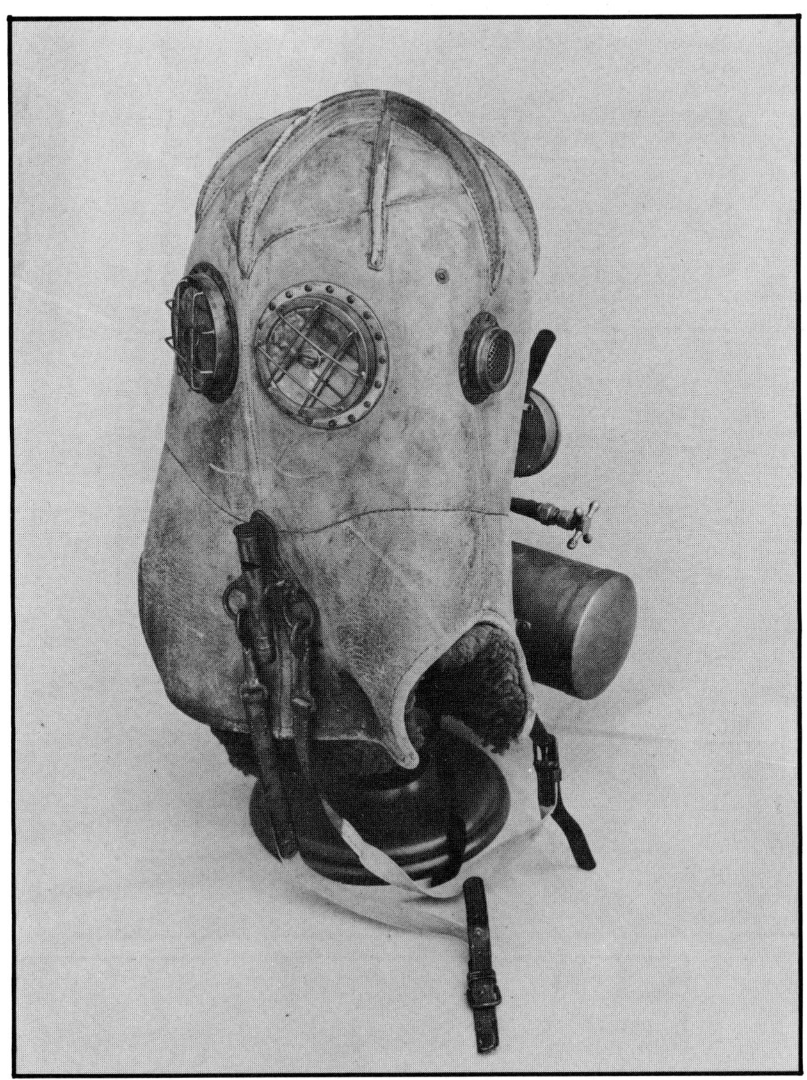

This is a "Vajens" Smoke Mask. It is a leather hood that was fitted over a firefighter's head and held in position with two armstraps. The metal canister on the back of the mask was pumped up to hold pressure and the valve on the back kept closed until the firefighter entered the building. The supply of air was very limited. It is estimated that this unit was made in the late 1800's.

FIRE MUSEUMS

When you get involved in collecting toys, you soon realize that you will probably never own all of the ones that have been produced. Realizing that limitation many collectors do like you are now. They begin to document what they have in their collections and try to locate examples of other specimens in other collections. Sort of like bird watching I guess . . . In other words "If you can't have one, the next best thing is to be able to see one."

One of the best ways to engage in that form of "collecting" is to visit museums and see what toys are in the collections.

At first blush the place to look would be Fire Museums. Most major cities have a fire museum located in the vicinity, especially those located in the East. If you really want to make a study of fire museums, the best resource to use is "The Visiting Fireman". This is a publication that annually prints a directory of fire museums as well as having a lot of information on fire buff groups and information on literature and items to buy to further your collection. The address of The Visiting Fireman is 1024 Elizabeth Street, Naperville, Illinois 60540.

However, there are several other museums that should never be overlooked as a potential source of information on toy and model fire apparatus. These are the Museums of Science and Industry and, of course, Toy Museums. A classic example of the types of experiences you can have in the Science museum can be found in the London Museum of Science and Industry. While preparing material for use in Volume three of this series I was privileged to go to that part of the world to visit. In that museum is an entire section that is devoted to fire apparatus . . . including many models of equipment. One of the models, for example, was a working model of a Newsham Hand pumper. Unfortunately, the photos taken on that trip were not finished in time to be included in this book. But, the point is look into the museums that focus on technology and especially the steam era and you may find some excellent toys and models.

The second type of museum seems so obvious . . . Toy museums. But, a lot of people discount toy museums because they tend towards dolls and such. They tend to be very specialized and very few specialize in fire truck toys. Nonetheless, they need to be explored carefully. During the research for this book I visited the Atlanta Toy Museum and was delighted by the exhibits there. In another case I spent four hours exploring a toy museum and only found one fire truck . . . but it was a beauty. It was a clockwork tin and was just "setting there."

In summary, one of the best ways of collecting toys is to find them in their natural habitat . . . the collection. Visit every museum that you have the opportunity to and you will be surprised at how many toys you will be able to add to your vocabulary . . .

Lewis chief 1929

THE HOME OF A TYPICAL FIRE MEMORBILLIA COLLECTOR

Does this look familiar? It is typical of what Ray and I see as we travel about visiting different collectors. There are two things that really stick out about serious collectors. The first is that their collections are almost always impeccably neat . . . the second is that they can find almost anything in the collection in moments. Everything has a place and everything is in its place.

PENNY TOY, made in 1972 in Italy. The material is die cast metal with plastic parts. It is a copy of an Esadelta Fire Engine. The number is 117. The scale is 1/56. Overall length is 4".

MFG. UNKNOWN, made in England in the late 1930's. These toys were cast lead. Overall height is about 3".

PHOENIX MFG. This toy was made in England in the 1980's and was cast in pewter. The dimensions are about 4" high. The piece depicts Victorian era firefighters. This piece also came painted and was part of a series.

PILEN, made in Spain of die cast metal in 1983.
Serial number is 307. The doors open on this
representation of an Oldsmobile Toranado Fire
Chief's car. Length is 4''.

PILEN, made in 1978, Spanish, die cast metal.
This toy is a copy of a Range Rover Fire Vechicle.
The words on the door read ''Jefe Bomberos,''
which means Chief of the Fire Department. The
Beacon is amber. Length is 4''.

This model was a kit bash of a Revell ZIS-6 kit.
It is a Russian Ladder truck that uses both the
Revell parts and some scratch-built parts. The
The overall length is about 6''.

MFG. UNKNOWN, made in Japan about 1950.
The material is pressed tin. It seems to be a copy
of a 1950 era GMC Pumper. The total length is 6½''.

PLASTICVILLE, INC., made in U.S.A. in 1965.
No serial number. Made of injection molded plastic.
Approximately 5.5'' long. The toy looks like an
American LaFrance Ladder Truck. The truck can
be used with a model railroad fire station.

PLASTICVILLE, INC., made in the U.S.A. in 1965.
No serial number. Made of injection molded plastic.
Approximately 5.5'' long. The toy looks like an
American LaFrance engine. The truck can be used
with a model railroad fire station.

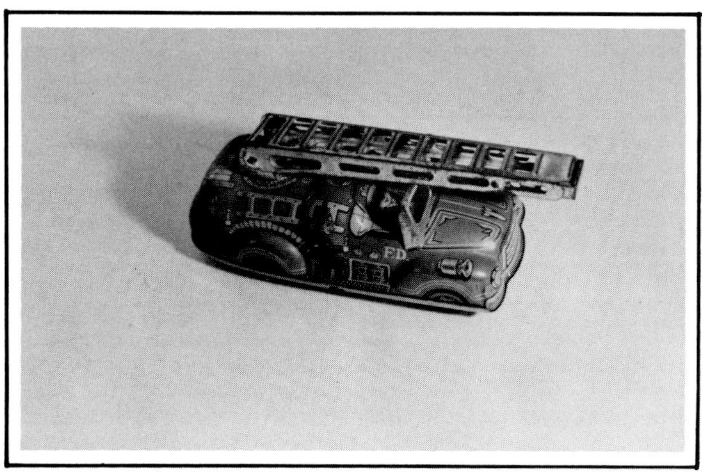

MFG. UNKNOWN, made in Japan in 1955. Made of pressed tin. Approximately 4.5'' long. Motor has friction drive. Note it has an American fireman painted on the vehicle.

PLAYART, made in 1981, Hong Kong, die cast metal. This toy has a metal body and plastic windows and wheels. The overall dimensions are 2¾''.

PLAYART, made in the 1980's. This is a diecast toy with some plastic parts, made in Hong Kong. The truck has a decal on the side of the apparatus that says Baltimore Fire Department. Yet the decal on the front of the engine says "EFD". The decal on the door says Truck Company 26. Apparently Playart only had one set of decals for the two models they put out. Model number 7968. Overall length 7¾".

PLAYART, made in the 1980's. This is a diecast toy with some plastic parts. Made in Hong Kong. The truck has a decal on the side of the apparatus that says Baltimore Fire Department. Yet the decal on the front of the engine says "EFD". The decal on the door says Truck Company 26. Overall length is 6". Model number 7969.

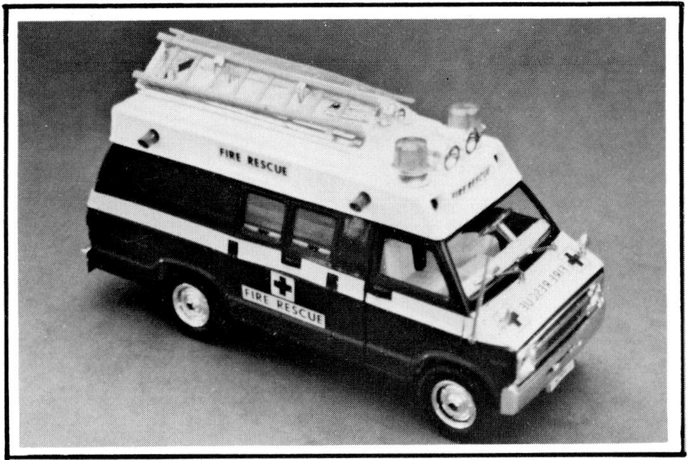

POLISTIL, made in Italy in 1980. The material is die cast metal with small plastic parts. It is a copy of Dodge Van Ambulance of the type used in the U.S.A. The total length is 6¼".

PRALINE, made in 1983 of injection molded
plastic. Made in West Germany. This toy was an
advertising gimmick for a magazine called "Der
Feuerwehr." (Fire and Water). Overall length
is approximately 2". Note that this toy is based
on an apparatus design with only three wheels.

PRALINE, made in 1983 of injection molded
plastic. This is a toy that was developed as an
advertising gimmick for a magazine called "Fire
and Water". The toy was made in West Germany.
Overall length 2¼".

PREISER, made in West Germany, made in 1980.
Serial number 2631. Approximate length 5.25".
Made of injection molded plastic. The toy comes
as a kit or a build up. It looks like a faun crash
truck used in Europe. It discharges foam through
large nozzle on the top of the truck.

·PREP, made in Germany in 1983 of molded
plastic. Fashioned after a Mercedes Benz fire
car. The length is 2''.

RAJ INDUSTRIES
made in India in 1978. Made of pressed
tin. No serial number. Approximate length 7''.
Motor is clockwork engine. There is detailed painting of firemen fighting fire. Also notes other fire
scenes —unofficially called India Tin.

RAJ INDUSTRIES
India 1978. Made of pressed tin. No serial
number. Approximately 7'' long. Motor is clockwork engine. There is detailed painting of firemen
fighting fire. Also notes other fire scenes — unoffi-
cally called India Tin.

MFG. UNKNOWN, made in Japan in the early 1960's. Stamped tin. Plastic headlights and rubber tires. Friction motor powered. Length is 6½". Very fine looking toy.

MFG. UNKNOWN, made in Japan in the 1950's of pressed tin. This toy was shown in Book one also, but in this version the firefighters are dressed in American fire equipment. Length is 6.5".

MFG. UNKNOWN, made in Czecholvakia during the pre-war era. The material is stamped metal. The toy was painted yellow on the top and the body, the engine cowl was red and the hose reels were green. No motor. Length is about 8".

 RALSTOY, made in the U.S.A. of die cast metal. They represent an air truck and a tactical command unit from the Miami and Newark Fire Departments. They both have the same serial number of 22 on them   Length is 4¼''.

RENWAL, made in 1950's in the United States. The material is die cast metal. These two also appear in volume 1 of this series. In volume 1 you will notice that they are made os acetate plastic. In this picture we have the die cast version. The pumper had the serial number 145. The ladder truck had the serial number 146. The total length was 3½'' on both vehicles. Another interesting thing about comparing the plastic and metal versions is that in the plastic version the windows are open and in the metal version they are closed.

REVELL, this toy was made in the U.S.A. around 1964. It was manufactured from injected molded plastic. There was no serial number on the toy. It was manufactured to the Ho scale. It was based on a New York Fire Boat that was used for many years in the New York Harbor.

RICHARD MODEL COMPANY, made in the late 1940's. This was a Balsa Wood kit. The kit came equipped with set of plans to construct. There was no serial number. The overall length of the toy was 7''. The model was based on a Pirsch Apparatus of that era.

ROCO, made in Austria in 1982 of molded plastic. A Steyr 91 TFLA Combination Water Truck and Crash Vehicle. The full sized version of this apparatus is made by Rosenbauer in Austria. Length is 3¼''.

ROCO, made in 1980 in Austria. This is a copy
of Pinzgauer All Wheel Drive Fire Engine . . .
the sign on the door indicates that it is used by
a volunteer fire department. The toy has a Volkswagen powered portable pump. The scale is about
1/87. The overall length is 2¼''.

ROCO, made in Austria, manufactured in 1980's.
Material is plastic. It is a copy of an Unimog Fire
Apparatus. The ladders come in a kit form to add
to the toy. The overall length is 2½''.

ROCO. Made in Austria in 1982. It is made of
injection molded plastic. There is jo serial number
on the toy. Its overall length is about 1½'' long.
It was patterned after the DBGM Jeep that is used
as a staff car. The top is removable from the toy.

ROCO, made in West Germany in 1982 of plastic.
German Fire Service Hauler on a Mann chassis.
The cover on the back comes off. Length is 3¼".

ROSKOPF. This toy was made in West Germany
in 1982. It is made of injection molded plastic.
The overall length of the toy is 1½". There is no
serial number. It is based on the type of Volkswagen
that is used as a staff and command vehicle in the
German Fire Service. On this toy the roof comes off.

MFG. UNKNOWN. This is the smallest toy I've
been able to locate. This one is in the collection
of a Fire Chief up in Alaska. Considering the size
of that state I was surprised that the smallest fire
truck would show up there.

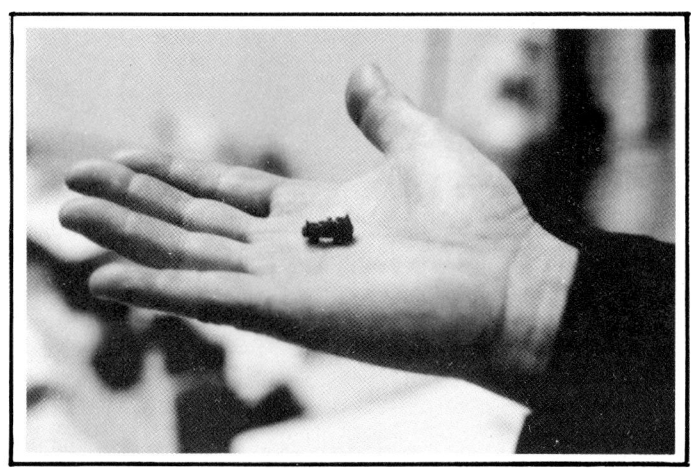

MFG. UNKNOWN, made in the United States, Era 1952-54. Made of lead. The toy is a copy of the American LaFrance 85 foot Aerial Ladder of that era. It was sold originally as an addendum to a model railroad set, so it is assumed that the scale is Ho Scale. The model is very detailed. The overall length is 5½".

MFG. UNKNOWN, ERa 1945-50. The toy is made of plastic. The unit is missing a portion of a ladder. It is a copy of an older style American LaFrance, Pirsch or Seagrave. Overall Length 5".

MFG. UNKNOWN, era 1914. Made in the United States. The material is glass, with a metal bottom and metal wheels. This is a copy of one of the transition pieces from Horse Drawn to the Motorized Steamer. The actual date of manufacture was Nov. 4, 1914. The total length is 5".

SAKURA, made in Japan in 1981. This is a die
cast metal toy. It has no serial number and is about
4" overall in length. It is based on the Toyota Crown
Fire Chief's vechicle. It has a battery powered motor
and a red flashing light.

SAKURA, made in Japan in 1980. Made of die
cast metal. Serial number 4074. Approximately
4" long. Resembles a Toyota Japanese Fire
Vehicle and has an operating red light.

SAKURA, made in Japan in 1980. Made of die
cast metal. No serial number. Approximately 4"
long. The car resembles a Japanese Staff car. The
car features an operating red light.

SAKUARA PET, made in Japan in 1980. The material is die cast metal. It is a copy of a Toyota Type Pumper. The total length is 4''.

ARNOLD, pressed tin made in Great Britain in the 1950's. The device with the crank was used to move the vehicle. The overall dimensions were about 7''.

MFG. UNKNOWN, made in Japan, era 1950's. The material is tin. It is a very large model. When the truck is bumped in the front, the ladder raises. It is run on friction. Overall length is about 13''.

MFG. UNKNOWN, made in U.S.A. in the 1950's. These toys may be Keystone, but we are not sure. The length is 3''. These were made in a variety of colors.

MFG. UNKNOWN, made in Taiwan in about 1980 or 1981. The toy was pressed tin with no serial number. The overall length was about 10½''. It represents a Mercedes Benz fire chief's car. The toy was battery operated and when turned on the red light on the top blinked.

SCOTT MORELAND RECASTINGS. These toys are a recasting of the Revell Kits. Scott Moreland has taken the horses from a Britain Limited Kit, the Dalmatians from a Trophy casting. The figures have had new heads cast on them too.

SFTF TOYS, made in Mainland China in 1980. Made of pressed tin. Serial number MF 183. Approximately 8'' long. Features a motor with friction drive.

SHACKMAN, made of glass in Taiwan in the 1970's. A reproduction of an early toy candy container.

MFG. UNKNOWN, made in Japan in the early 1960's. Made of pressed tin, rubber tires and friction motor. 7'' in length.

HERO TOY, made in Japan of pressed tin. The toy has a wind-up motor on the left side. The overall length is 3 3/8''. Era unknown.

SHUCO, ade in the mid seventies in West Germany. The material is die cast metal. It is a copy of an Audi 80. The serial ID is TYP. The scale is 1/66 scale. Overall length is about 2½... The front doors on this model open.

SIKU, made in Germany in 1979. The material is die cast metal with some plastic parts. It is a copy of a Unimog Mercedes Benz Airport Crash Rig. The box located inside carries extra rope and cable. The lights on the back extend upwards. The trailer is 3'' long, the main vehicle about 5'' long. The compartment doors open on both sides. The winch is manually operated.

SIKU, made in Germany in the late 1970's. The material is die cast metal. It has two identification numbers 1028 and 1322. It is a copy of a Ford-Granada Turnier. In the rear of this vehicle is a box that contains several traffic cones. Overall length is 3¼".

SIKU, made in Germany about 1954. The material is plastic. It is a copy of a Mercedes Benz Metz. The scale is 1/48th. Overall length is 5¼". It is the companion piece to the Mercedes Benz Pumper toy of that same era, see page

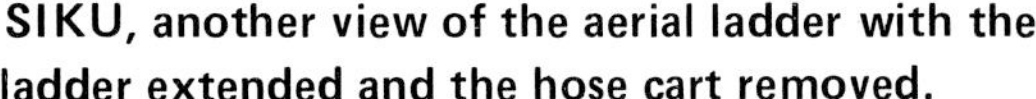

SIKU, another view of the aerial ladder with the ladder extended and the hose cart removed.

SIKU, made in 1976 in West Germany. Diecast molded of metal. Approximate length 3.5''. A German ambulance on the Mercedes Benz L408D chassis. Has opening doors and stretcher is removable. No serial number.

SIKU, made in 1980 in West Germany. The material is die cast metal. It has complete interior. It is a cover of Range-Rover Vehicle. There is no serial number. The overall length is about 3''.

SIKU, made in West Germany in 1983 of die cast metal. The serial number is 1044. Represents a Mercedes Benz 280 GE Staff car. Length is 3''.

SIKU, made in Germany about 1955. Material is plastic. This model was shown in Volume one, but we did not show the various pieces of equipment that comes with it. See Volume one, page The scale is 1/48th. The total length is 5¼''.

SMITH MILLER TOYS, made of pressed steel in the U.S.A. in the 1950's. A very, very sturdily built toy.

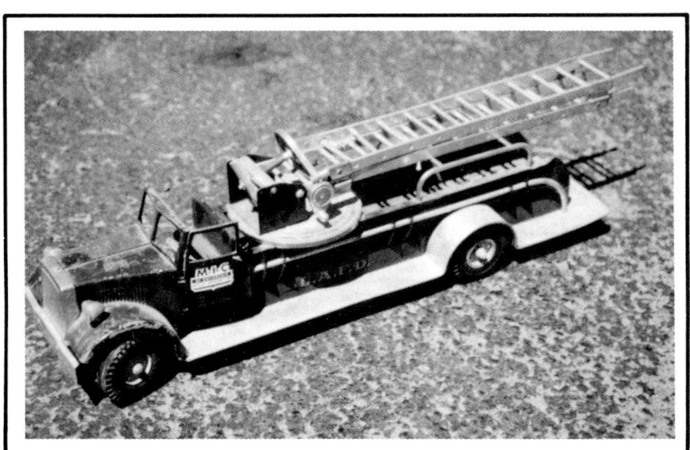

SMITH MILLER, made in the United States in the 1950's. This is a pressed steel truck of a very rugged construction. Overall length is about 3½ feet.

SMITH AUTO MODELERS, made in England in 1980. It is a die cast metal. It is a copy of a Daf - 2000 Fire Tender. This particular model features the ladder that was used on the early Dinky Models. The body comes in both silver and red. Overall length is 5½".

A SMITH MODEL from England. The red body versus the silver body.

MFG. UNKNOWN, made in about 1970 in Japan. The material is die cast metal. The firemen on this toy have the traditional garb of that era. The horses are not permanently attached to the apparatus. The overall length is 2". The horses about 1" long.

MFG. UNKNOWN, made in Taiwan in 1980 of die cast metal. Patterned after a Hodge fire steamer used in the U.S.A. in 1840. Sold as a pencil sharpener. Length 2¾".

MFG. UNKNOWN, made in Japan of Pressed tin. Overall length 3½".

MFG. UNKNOWN, made in Japan in the 1970's.
The truck is made of plastic and tin. The toy was
battery operated and the truck could be made to go
right, left and forward and reverse. The platform
elevates. There was no serial number. The overall
length was 16''.

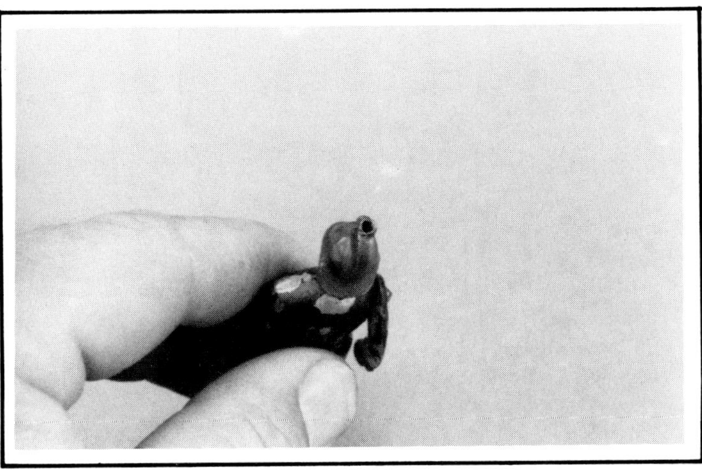

THE "SPRUE" from the casting of toy firefighters.
This is the opening where the lead or pewter is
poured into the mold. In some castings the sprue
hole is ground off and in some cases filled in to
make the toy look better. Usually the sprue is on
the bottom of the toy.

MFG. UNKNOWN, made in Hong Kong.
Made of pressed tin and plastic. The toys
were unique in that they appeared to be
placed in a plastic "Conveyance" that must
have housed other models also. When the clock
work motor was operated the metal portion
bounced up and down. Note the ladders on one
truck were yellow and the other red. The markings on the door say "Fire Chief"

SN TOYS, made in Japan in the 1950's. It is made of pressed tin. The serial number is A4234. Overall length is 7¼". The toy is friction driven.

SOLIDO, made in France in 1980. Material is die cast metal. It is a copy of a Puegot J7, a vehicle that is commonly used as an ambulance. It is in the scale of 1/50. The overall length is 31/2".

SOLIDO, made in 1981 in France. The material is die cast metal with some plastic parts. This is one of the last toys made by Solido as it was being purchased by Majorette. It is a model of the 1930 Citroen C4F. Scale is 1/43. No serial number. Overall length is 3½". The model is still being produced by Majorette.

SOLIDO, made in France in 1979 of die cast metal.
Some plastic parts. Serial number is 366. A Saviem
SG4 Fast Attack or First Aid Fire Appliance. Overall
length is 4½″. The ladders and hose reels are removable.

SOLIDO, made in France in 1979. The material is die
cast metal. It is a copy of a Jeep Radio Vechicle pulling a portable pump. The top of the portable pump is
removable for use as a sump. The scale is 1/43. The
serial number is number 256 in the Solido series. The
trailer is number 360. The jeep is 3″ long and the
trailer is 2″ long.

SOLIDO, made in France in 1980. Material is die
cast metal. It is a copy of a Berlia Gak-17. It is in
the scale of 1/55. It is known as a Fourgon-Mixte.
The total length is 4″.

SSS INTERNATIONAL, made in Japan in the late
1950's. The material is tin. The serial number is
S-1068. The outriggers work and the ladder extends
and elevates with a hand crank. The overall dimensions of the toy are 17¾".

STARLUX, made in France in 1980. These
are injection molded plastic that are then hand
painted. This set is in the 1/48 scale. This represents a French Water Rescue Team.

FIREFIGHTER WITH A CO2 EXTINGUISHER
AND FIREFIGHTER WITH A RADIO.

HYDRANT MAN AND ROPE MAN

NOZZLEMAN AND LIGHTMAN

AXEMAN AND PUMPMAN

HOSEMAN AND FIREFIGHTER IN BREAHTING APPARATUS

FIREFIGHTER WITH GRAPPLING HOOK AND ROPE

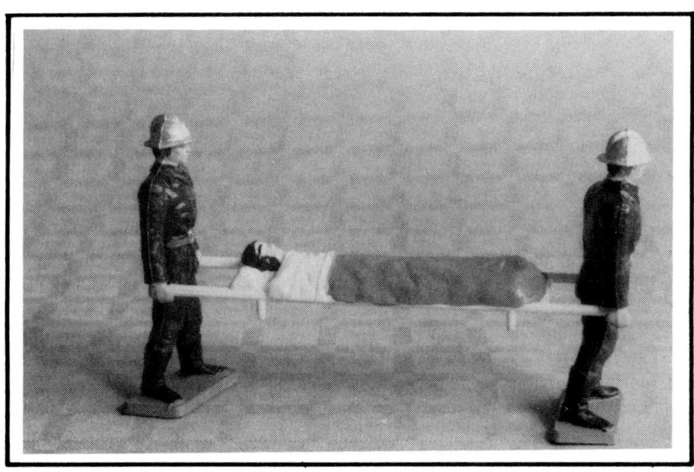

STRETCHER MEN

STARLUX , made in France in 1952. These toys are made by pouring a composition material into the mold and then applying pressure. These are 1/48 scale. There are 2 sets of 5 pieces each. The first set has four firefighters and a fire alarm box. The second set has five firefighters.

MFG. UNKNOWN, made in the U.S.A. between 1945 and 1950. Wooden material. Overall length was 8''. A typical "Pull Toy".

STROMBECKER TOY, made in the U.S.A. of injection molded plastic, unknown date. The toy was very cheaply made and the finish is very typical of "throw away" toys. Original cost was bout $1.15. Overall length is about 5½".

SUMMER CORP., made in Hong Kong in 1983. Serial number S8114. Approximately 4" long. Patterned after a Japanese Aerial Ladder. The ladder raises and extends.

SUMMER TOYS, made in Hong Kong in 1980 of die cast metal. Serial number S8113. Patterned after the British ERF Fire Tender and Pump Escape. Length is 4¼".

SUMMER TOYS, made in Hong Kong in 1980 of die cast metal. Serial number is S8116. Based on the Isusu Pumper of Japan. Length is 3 4/4''.

SUMMER TOYS, made in Hong Kong in 1980 of die cast metal. Serial number is S8115. Japanese Crash Fire Rig. Length is 4''.

TANDY-RADIO SHACK. Made in Hong Kong in about 1979. The toy is made of injection molded plastic. Its overall length is about 11¼'' long. The toy is battery operated.

TEKNO, made in Denmark between 1945-50. Pressed tin and die cast metal construction. No serial number. The overall length is 6".

TEKNO, made in Denmark in 1958. The toy is die cast metal. The serial number is 415. It is patterned after a Taunus Transit Rescue truck. The overall length is 4".

TEKNO TOY, made in Denmark in the early 60's. No serial number. Approximately 4" long. Made of die cast metal. Patterned after a VW Pickup Pumper. Note: Also listed in Volume one with hose reels in back. This is a variation.

MFG. UNKNOWN, made in West Germany in the 1950's. It is made of wood with rubber tires. The overall length is about 24''. A very large pull toy. The ladder operates in two sections.

MFG. UNKNOWN, made in the 1960's in Japan. The material is pressed tin. Friction motor powered. Length is about 7''.

MFG. UNKNOWN, made of pressed tin. This shot was made at a Toy Show and no details were available on the two pieces and the station. We have been told that the pieces were German and from the 1920's. I can't prove it one way or the other.

THOMAS, made in the U.S.A. of plastic. The
toy has a serial number on the inside of the roof
of I-140. Under that number is an 8. The ladder
bracket is metal. There is a hole in the tailboard
to tow something. The time period is probably in
the 1950's. The overall length is 4'' to end of
tailboard.

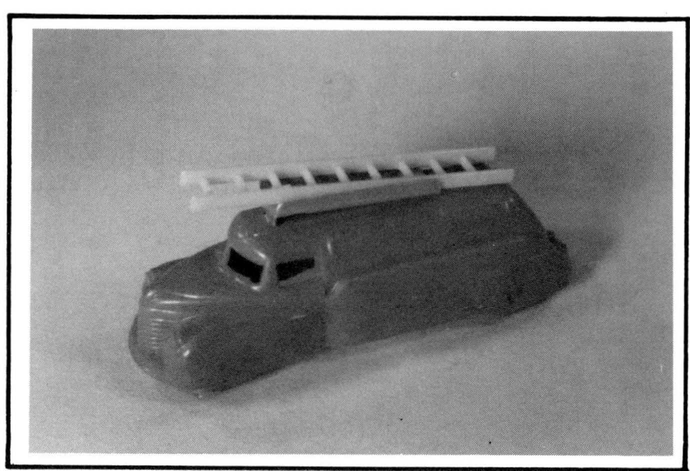

TM MODERN TOYS, made in Japan in the late
1960's. The toy is made of tin. It has a battery
and a remote control that operates the ladder.
The truck would move forward and the siren would
operate. The overall dimensions are 13¾''.

TN TOYS, made in Hong Kong in the 1980's
of injection molded plastic. Overall length is
about 5½''.

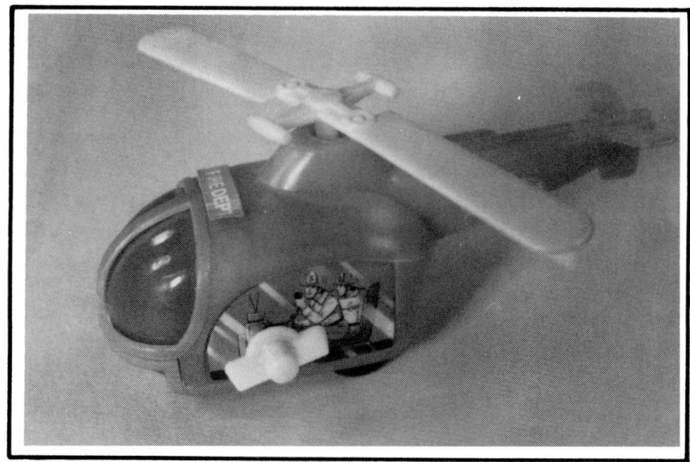

TOMIKA, made in 1981 in Japan. The material
is die cast metal. The serial number is 2. The scale
is 1/43. It is based onthe Hino Aerial Ladder. This
is a Tomika "Dandy", overall length 8½". The
unit is very heavy, very fine decalling. The cost of
this toy when brand new is $30.00.

Shows the TOMIKA No.2 with the jacks down and
the ladder extended. This type of Aerial is very
popular in Japan due to the fact the front wheels
make it more manueverable.

TOMIKA, made in Japan in 1981. The material is
die cast metal. The serial number is 5. It is a copy
of a Nissan Diesel Chemical Engine. The scale is 1/58.
The unique thing about this toy is the Japanese writing
and the elephant on the door squirting water with its
trunk. The total length is 4½".

TOMIKA, made in 1980, Japan. The material
is die cast metal with plastic parts. It is a copy
of a Izuzu TKD-23F Fire Engine. It's a "Dandy"
style toy which is a larger scale of a toy. The
model number is 46. The scale is 1/56. The
overall length is about 4". Tomika also makes
this model in a smaller version, 1/87th scale.

TOMIKA, made in Japan in 1978. The toy is die
cast metal. The serial number is F-35. Patterned
after an American LaFrance remounted aerial
apparatus. The overall length is 3".

TOMIKA, made in Japan in about 1981. The material
is die cast metal. It is a copy of a Citroen H Type Van.
The scale is 1/48. This is the "Dandy" scale. The length
is about 4". This particular toy is redesigned from
another toy that was not originally a fire truck.

TOMIKA, made in Japan in 1979. The material is a die cast body, with a plastic snorkel boom and basket. The nozzles are metal. The unit is a copy of a Hino Fire Apparatus presently in use in Japan. The scale is 1/82. The identification number is 37. Overall length is 4½''.

TOMIKA, made in Japan in 1979. The material is die cast metal. The scale is 1/110th. The identification number is L10. It is a copy of an American-LaFrance Aerial Ladder. On the door of the unit it states LaCounty 31. Very detailed model. Not readily available in the United States except through toy dealers.

TONKA TRUCKS

Of all the toy fire trucks that have been manufactured, none is more well known to the toy consuming public than the TONKA. It has grown to be synomous with "sturdy, well-built". From a standpoint of the toy fire truck collector, it is not recognized as being one of the more accurate representations of real apparatus. In both cases however, the TONKA has provided a real contribution to the toy market. The company that produced the TONKA has consistently produced a quality toy that is both enduring and enjoyable to have in a complete toy collection.

The following information on the TONKA line of toy fire apparatus is derived from a listing of catalogues that the authors were fortunate enough to obtain from a fire prevention education officer from the Minnesota area. Hopefully the information from these various years will help you identify and catalogue your toys.

1955 — In 1955 the Mound Metalcraft, Inc. Toy Manufacturers produced the first "Tonka." The first piece illustrated in the catalogue was : 700-5 AERIAL LADDER TRUCK.

It was described as "Exciting, realistic detail in every inch of this big scale model of the popular "Hook and Ladder." Tillermans seat swings out of the way for ladder operation. Smooth plated crank on simulated hydraulic raising mechanism lifts ladder to proper position and extends it. Length 32½", height 7¼", width 6". Originally packed four to a shipper. Weight 42½ lbs.

The specifications for the toy included 20 guage steel with Dupont "Dulux" enamel paint. The decals on the toy were "MFD".

1956 — In this year the TONKA went to a complete fire department. The catalogue lists a "Complete three vehicle Fire Department." Includes the aerial ladder, suburban pumper plus Emergency Rescue Squad truck and metal fire chief's badge. Set was individually packed, weight of 21½ lbs.

The various apparatus were described as "Big, realistic aerial ladder. Heavy, rugged and true to life in appearance and action. Aluminum ladder is raised and extended by simulated hydraulic control to a big 36" height. Ladder base revolves full 360 degrees. Truck carries two extra auxiliary ladders."

"Suburban Pumper with real hydrant . . . Engine connects to a miniature hydrant (included) that connects to a garden hose for real operation. Hydrant regulates water flow through pumper and fire hose. Pumper carries removable ladders, two, six inch rubber, hydrant hoses and a forty inch fire hose. Hose has hook for attaching to the aerial ladder if desired." The length of the Suburban was 17", height 6½", width 6". It originally came packed four to a shipper in the weight of 23½ lbs.

The Rescue Squad was not described separately in the catalogue.

The interesting thing about the toys was that the decals went from "MFD" to "TFD".

1957 — The catalogue now shows the same three pieces sold separately. This time the catalogue describes the rescue truck as having: "brilliant markings and a simulated flasher light and siren all add to excitement and realism of this emergency vehicle. The rescue truck has a sliding side door and full size rear doors which means the big interior can be loaded with rescue equipment."

The rescue van was painted white as in the previous year and the decals were Tonka Fire Department. The number 5 was on the side of the truck. The dimensions noted in the catalogue were 12" long, 7½" high and 5½" wide. They were packed six to a shipper at a weight of 24 lbs.

The catalogue number was 24 and the rescue sold for $4.98 when new.

The suburban pumper was now given the catalogue number of 46. A "realistic" wrench was now part of the kit (no mention of the badge). The removable ladder was noted to be 10½" long. The sale price was $8.98.

The aerial ladder was now given the catalogue number of 48. The one removable ladder was noted to be 19" long. The cost was $12.98.

The kit was available as catalogue number B0212. It was described as "the most complete, workable and thoroughly appealing Fire Department set ever assembled in one big handsome display package." The set included the metal badge and an additional ladder was added to the aerial when it was in the kit. The set boxed had the dimensions of 33" long, 17¾" wide and 6¼" high. (That must have been a biggy under the Christmas tree). The cost of the kit was $27.95.

1958 — In 1958 the rescue truck disappears from the catalogue. The aerial ladder goes to $13.98 cost and the suburban pumper goes for $9.98.

The kit for this year shows a Tanker as part of the Department inventory. The kit sold for $29.95. The badge is still in the kit, but the tanker does not appear to be sold separately.

1959 — The catalogue cover features the aerial ladder and a young boy with a helmet numbered No. 1.

The variations really start this year. For starters the suburban pumper is painted white and the price has gone back to $8.98. The aerial ladder remains unchanged but once again the aerial sold along has only one ladder. The catalogue page with the fire apparatus has a youngster on a ladder quoting: "When I'm a man I'll be a fireman stout;
I'll go to all the fires and put them out."

There were two kits for this year. The first kit for this year shows both the pumper and the suburban painted white. Also, the kit only has two pieces in it. It's hard to say whether both ladders were in the kit from the photo, but the description reads "with auxillary ladders" so we assume the plural. The ladder was disconnected and the overall package dropped to a dimension of 30¼" long by 16" wide and 6½" high. The price came way down to $21.95.

The second kit, catalogue number B-225 shows the apparatus painted red. The third piece in this set is a "rescue" truck, painted white. It appears to be a recycled version of the catalogue number 05 "Sportsman". This vehicle is a pickup with a camper, a siren and light flasher and a plastic rescue boat on the top. This kit sold for $25.95.

1960 — The suburban is now sold for $8.98. The aerial ladder is now $12.98 but no TONKA FIRE DEPT. The kit doesn't appear in this years catalogue.

1961 — The rescue squad appears as catalogue number 105. It is described as having white sidewall tires. Dimensions are 13¾" long, 7¼" high and 5¼" wide. The toy sold for $3.98. The suburban is still available for $8.98 and the aerial ladder is still $12.98. This obviously was pre-inflation! No kit in this year either.

1962 — The catalogue number of the pumper now reads 926. The aerial ladder is now catalogue number 1398. The prices of both toys went up .02. Not much inflation that year either!

1963 — This year sees the introduction of the "Jeep Pumper". It is catalogue number 425. It is described as: "unusually low price for this remarkably life-like toy. (unusual statement in view of the fact that there was not a counterpart in the real fire world of this truck). Hose, which pulls out of the tank, squirts water when pumper is connected to garden hose. Equipment includes emergency light, steering wheel, detachable ladder, trailer hitch, hand rail, two fire extinguishers. The dimensions are 10¾" long, 6¼" high, 5¼" wide. Packed six to a shipper at a weight of 15 lbs. The cost $4.00."

1964 — The pumper retained the catalogue number of 926 but the aerial ladder changed again to a new number 998. The '64 catalogue mentions the "Mini-Tonka" line that was "introduced in 1963" but there is no mention of fire apparatus in the mini series.

1965 — The "Jeep Pumper" is still available as catalogue number 425. The 926 pumper and the aerial ladder (now back to 998) undergo a "nose job" with new front ends. The bobbed-off noses look more like the cab-over design than the older design. The truck now has white sidewalls. There is a MINI-TONKA series in the 65 catalogue, but no mention of fire apparatus.

1966 — Not a good year for fire trucks. The 926 pumper is there and so is the 998 aerial ladder . . . but that's it!

1967 — Aha . . . catalogue number 66 . . . The FIRE CHIEF. A station wagon apparatus "complete with spring-action tailgate, red flasher, steel construction, enamel finish." The vehicle has a decal that reads "FIRE CHIEF". Front and rear seats. Overall length is 9 1/8", 3 3/8" wide, 4 1/8" high. Shipped twelve to a shipper, total weight 13 lbs.

The Suburban pumper is no longer alone! The "FIREFIGHTER" is catalogue number 72. It no longer has the hydrant and the hose reels. The new reels are molded plastic. The decal says Tonka, not TFD. The rear tires are duals. Overall length is 9¾", 4 1/8" wide and 4½" high. The two ladders on each side are detachable.

And guess what's back . . . the Fire Department kit. It is catalogue number 103. It contains the FIREFIGHTER pumper, the FIRE CHIEF car and the JEEP pumper. Overall kit dimensions are 12 3/16" long, 5 9/16" high and 10 1/8" wide. The Suburban No. 926 and the Aerial ladder No. 998 are still in the catalogue. No change in specifications.

1968 — The Tiny Tonkas arrive. The Tiny Tonka pumper is designated No. 595. It is made of steel with plastic ladders and hose bed. The overall dimensions are 5 13/16" long, 2½" high and 2 1/8" wide.

The FIRE CHIEF vehicle is numbered 1066 in this catalogue. The Mini-Tonka FIREFIGHTER is numbered 1072 in this catalogue. The Fire Department kit is available as number 1103 in this catalogue. The Suburban, with the cab-over design is now designated as 2926 in the catalogue. The Aerial ladder is now designated as 2998.

1969 — The Tiny Tonka pumper is still No. 595. The Tiny Tonka aerial is still No. 675. The Fire Chief is still 1066 and the Firefighter pumper is still 1072. The kit is still 1103.

The Suburban pumper has been remodeled. It is described as: "restyled completely for 1969. It includes a new style crew cab, shoots water stream from turret mounted deluge gun when hydrant is hooked to outside garden hose. Miniature hydrant wrench controls flow. Carries hydrant hoses on one side, removable ladders on the other. Full glassed-in" cab with detailed interior. New modern extra wide tires, steel body and baked truck enamel finish. Overall dimensions 17 1/8" long, 7¼" high and 5 15/16" wide. The same chassis was used to construct the SNORKEL PUMPER. This unit, identified by the No. 2950 in the catalogue was patterned after a real apparatus. The aerial platform raises and lowers with a lever. The overall length was 17 1/8", the height was 9 3/8" and the width was 5 5/16". The aerial ladder is still designated No. 2998.

1970 — Tiny Tonka's number 595 and 675 are still available. The Firefighter is still No. 1072. The modern Suburban pumper is found as No. 2820 in the catalogue. The Snorkel is No. 2950, the aerial is still 2998.

1971 — Numbers 595 and 675 still are there in the Tiny Tonkas. The Tiny Tonkas have a new FIRE DEPT. The kit was designated No. 830 and consisted of "a pumper, red pickup, hook and ladder, white ambulance and red fire chiefs car. 11½" long, 2 5/8" high and 8 5/8" wide.

TONKA, made in the United States in the 1950's.
The material is pressed steel. It is a copy of a Jeep
Fire Truck that was common to forestry or industrial
fire departments of that era. The length is about 7''.

TONKA, made in the U.S.A. in the 1960's. The kit
was 13 x 7½ x 7 in dimension.

TONKA, made in the U.S.A. in 1958. The toy was
of pressed steel and was very large, almost 32''
in length.

TONKA TOYS, INC , made in the U.S.A. in 1975 of pressed steel. Overall dimensions 11''.

TONKA TOYS, INC., made in the U.S.A. in 1975 of pressed steel. Length is about 6''.

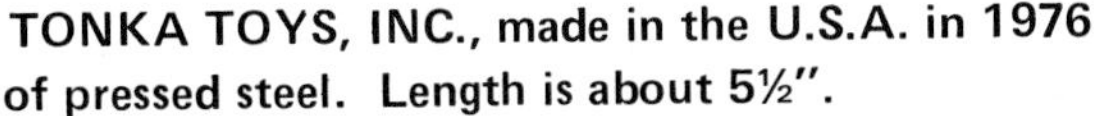

TONKA TOYS, INC., made in the U.S.A. in 1976 of pressed steel. Length is about 5½''.

TOOTSIE TOY, made in the U.S.A. in 1954. Serial number 2. Made of die cast metal. The working boom on this truck operates. The apparatus looks like a Mack truck. Overall length is 4½''.

TYCO, made in Hong Kong in 1983. Injection molded plastic. No serial number. This toy was used on a slot car track. Length is 3½''.

UK, made in Hong Kong in 1978. It is made of injection molded plastic. There is no serial number on the toy. Its overall length is about 14''. It is battery operated.

MFG. UNKNOWN, made in Japan in 1960. No serial number. Approximately 4.5" long. Made of pressed tin. The toy looks like a VW Bug Fire car. It features a friction motor.

MFG. UNKNOWN, made in the U.S.A. in 1948-1950. No serial number. Approximately 5" long. Made of cast glass. This was a candy container. There have been many glass fire engines made, most of them resemble older fire apparatus.

WIKING, made in West Germany, made in 1981.
The material is plastic. It is a copy of a Mercedes
Benz station wagon, 4 wheel drive utilized in most of
Europe as a chief officers vehicle or an emergency
rescue vehicle. In the back of this toy, made of plastic
also, are various pieces of rescue equipment. The
total length is 2''.

WIKING, made in West Germany in 1983.
Molded in plastic. Length is 2.0''. Based on
a German Crew Truck.

WIKING, made in West Germany in 1970's. It
is injection molded plastic. The overall length
is about 1¾''. It was patterned after the VW
Berlin-W Rescue Vehicle or Manpower Vehicle.

WIKING, made in West Germany in 1976. This is a plastic injection molded toy. The serial number is 27. The overall length of the toy is 2 3/8''. It is manufactured in the Ho scale. This toy represents a Mercedes Benz that is often used as a rescue unit and ambulance in the European Fire Service. This particular toy also comes equipped with a water rescue kit.

WIKING, made in West Germany in 1958. The toy was injection molded plastic. Patterned after the Mercedes Benz Metz German Ladder Truck. The serial number is 62. The overall length is 2''.

WIKING, made in West Germany in 1982. The toy was injection molded plastic. No serial number. The toy was patterned after the Mercedes Benz Ladder truck. The overall length was 3''.

WIKING, made in West Germany in 1980-81. The serial number on the toy is 631. Injection molded plastic. This Tow-Truck is about 1¼'' in length.

WIKING, made in West Germany in 1978. The toy was injection molded plastic. The serial number was 200. Patterned after the Mercedes Benz ambulance. The overall length was 2¼''.

WIKING, made in West Germany in 1977-78. Injection molded plastic. The serial number is 320. Was also used on the ''POLEZEI'' or Police Vehicle. The length is 1''.

WIKING, made in West Germany in 1968. Injection molded plastic. The serial number is 60W. This Rescue Van with the boat on top is 1¼″ in length.

WIKING, made in West Germany in 1982. Serial number 618. Approximately 2.5″ long. Made of injection molded plastic. The toy looks like a German Mercedes Metz Ladder Truck. The ladder raises and extends.

WIKING, made in West Germany in 1968. Injection molded plastic. A Mercedes Benz Staff Car. Overall length is 2″.

WIKING, made in West Germany in 1978. This is an injection molded plastic piece. The serial number is 631. The overall length of the toy is 2¼''. It is based on the International chassis that is used as a tow truck by the German Fire Service.

WIKING, made in West Germany in the late 1960's. The toy is injection molded plastic. There is no serial number. The overall length of the piece is about 3½''. This is manufactured in the Ho scale. The apparatus is patterned after the Mercedes Benz tow truck.

WIKING, made in 1981 in West Germany. The material is plastic. It is a copy of a Magirius KW-16 Crane. The scale is the normal 1/87 scale. Serial # Overall length is 3½''.

WILSON, made in the U.S.A. about 1930 of
pressed tin and wood. No serial number. The
clockwork motor runs the truck. The toy was
blue with red ladders. The ladder raises. The
length is 9''.

WANNATOYS, made in the U.S.A. in 1948 of
injection molded plastic. Serial number of 12.
Wheels are white. Length of toy is 4½''.

WINROSS, made in the U.S.A. in the 1960's. The toy is die cast metal. There is no serial number. The truck is patterned after a white MFG truck with a rescue body. The toy also came in the color white. The overall length was 3''.

WYANDOTTE, made in the U.S.A. in the early 1950's. The toy has a metal base, plastic body. The tires are rubber. The friction power motor makes a siren-like sound. Length is about 9¼''.

YANGMAN TOY COMPANY, made in Japan in 1972. The toy was made of pressed tin and some plastic. The overall length of the toy was about 10''. It was battery operated.

YATMING, made in the 1980's in England. It is
die cast metal. The Yatming truck was packaged as
part of a Fastwheels series. There were 12 in the
series. The Fire Truck is model 1356. Overall
length is 2 7/8''.

YONEZAWA, made in Japan in 1981. The toy
was die cast metal with a plastic ladder. There is
no serial number. It is patterned after the FUSO
Snorkel Fire Apparatus. The jacks extend with
the push of a button and the hose reel is retractable.
Overall length is 6''.

YONEZAWA TOYS, made in Japan. The toy was made
of die cast metal with some plastic parts. The toy was
manufactured in the 1/55 scale and is about 5½'' long
overall. It is patterned after the Iszu Truck Company.
The apparatus has a tilt cab and the doors open.

YONEZAWA TOYS, DIAPET made in the late
1970's or early 1980's. The material is die cast
metal with plastic aerial ladder. It is a copy of a
Hino Aerial ladder used in Japan. The scale 1/50.
The total length is 5½".

THE CLIMBING FIREMAN TOY. It was about
24 inches tall. Mfg. Unknown to us. This was
shot at a Toy Show and the information got mis-
placed. Anyone have any information on it?

MFG. UNKNOWN, made in France in 1960.
No serial number. Approximately 10" long.
Made of pressed tin, from sheet tin. It features
a jeep fire engine with tank trailer. It has a clockwork motor. The box that comes with this toy
is beautiful. It has several pictures of firemen
working, but no manufacturer name.

MFG. UNKNOWN, made in U.S.A. in 1948-1950.
No serial number. Made of molded rubber. Approximately 4.5" long. When toy is pressed it squeeks
like a toy mouse.

MFG. UNKNOWN (Written in Chinese) Made in
Mainline China in 1978. Made of pressed tin. Serial
number MS884. Approximately 5" long. The toy
looks like a jeep and has a clockwork engine.

MFG. UNKNOWN, made in Mainland,China in 1978.
Made of pressed tin. No serial number. Approximately
5.5" long. Features a friction motor drive.

A Frontpiece used by the New York Volunteer Association.

This is the type of ornamentation that was enbossed on the rear of the early firefighters helmets. The more of this type of labor that was used in the design of the helmet, the more expensive the helmet was.

MODEL, made in U.S.A. in 1982 of molded plastic. The length is 3¾'' and it simulates a French Brush Fire Truck made from a U.S. Army truck. Model made by Ray Russell.

158

BEAM WHISKEY BOTTLE. This is a whiskey bottle that was fabricated by the Jim Beam Company in the early 1980's. This one is patterned after a 1928 Fire Chief's car. In the original brochure it states—"With the advent of the Automobile age, the Fire Chiefs were the first to replace their buggies with a "Horseless Carriage", but the new machines were still called buggies.

Tradition dies hard. Refinements were added to the new buggies so that by the late twenties, a standard car like a Model "A Red" with gold striping on the doors, panels and fenders; red warning lights were added or substituted for the headlights. A bell mounted in a bracket was installed in front of the radiator with a bell cord extending through the fire wall to the front seat; an electric or flywheel operated siren was installed under the hood. 1928 Model "A" Ford Fire Chief cars came equipped with a black waterproof roof which could not be painted red, so it remained black.

Do you know some Beam Bottles have a trading value among collectors of over $3,000?

There exists more than 200 local Beam Bottle Clubs throughout the United States and five other nations. These clubs have affiliated to form the International Association of Jim Beam Bottles and Specialties Club. This Association was formed by the many Beam Collectors to further their fascinating hobby and promote their aims of fun, friendship and charity. Want to know more about it? Send a letter to:

INTERNATIONAL ASSOCIATION OF JIM BEAM BOTTLE AND SPECIALTIES CLUB
5120 Belmont Road, Suite D
Downers Grove, Illinois 60515
Attn: Mrs. Shirley Clark, Executive Secretary

BEAM WHISKEY BOTTLE, made in the early 1980's. Patterned after Steam Fire Apparatus. Overall length approximately 14". Overall height about 10".

This medal was struck by the Chicago Historical Society to commemorate the Great Chicago Fire of 1871. This medal was struck in 1971 on the Centennial. It is very heavy brass and is about 1½″ in diameter.

YONEZAWA TOYS (DIADET) made in Japan in the mid 1970's. The toys are die cast metal with some plastic parts. There is no serial number on the toy. The truck is patterned after the Toyota Hiaca ambulance used in Japan. The overall dimensions of the toy are 5¼″.

This Badge is rather unusual too. It was issued to
a doctor in Los Angeles in the 1930's or 1940's.
He was sort of a fire buff and lived in the San Fer-
nando Valley. He responded to so many fires that
the department made him the official "Surgeon".
Maybe he was the first Fire Department "Medic"
in Los Angeles.

MFG. UNKNOWN, made in the 1980's in
Taiwan. Made of pressed metal. This ia a
cheaper version of the Firetruck Christmas
ornament made by Hallmark. Overall length
about 3".

TN TOY, made in Japan of pressed tin. The toy
appears to be in the 1970's. The vehicle has a
license number of 6544. The overall length is 3½".

MFG. UNKNOWN. Plastic injection molded from the 1950's. Country of origin unknown. Push type toy.

MFG. UNKNOWN. Plastic injection molded from the 1950's. Country of origin unknown. It is battery powered and appears to be patterned after the Hudson Hornet. Overall dimensions about 9''.

This is a "Scratch-Built", or built from hand-built parts kit. It is an early Howe Apparatus designed to fight rural fires, or to respond to industrial fire brigade needs. It is about 4'' in length.

This MARX TOY appears in Book one, but we had a chance to shoot the box with this one so we added it to this volume also. For details on the era and dimension see Volume one, page 71.

MFG. UNKNOWN, made in Taiwan in about 1975. This reproduction is made of cast iron and represents an early Steamer. Length is 10".

The Fire Chiefs car in the Mini Series now has a white roof and is referred to as in the "Mini Tonka" HI-WAY PATROL AND FIRE CHIEFS CAR. The catalogue number is 1065.

The Fire truck is now called the "Super Thrust" Firefighter because the cab projects so far out. The catalogue number is 1255. The Tonka pumper is still No. 2820, the snorkel is 2950 and the aerial is 2998.

For those of you with a forest fire fighting interest this was the year that Tonka introduced the "Junior Forest Ranger Handbook" and the "Smokey Bear's Patrol kit". This five piece kit, catalogued as No. 5000, contained a Mini-Tonka jeep, a Smokey Bear, one ranger, a handbook, and iron-on Smokey Bear patch. The arms and heads are moveable on the bear and the forest ranger.

Kit number 5035 contained among other things a Mini-Tonka pickup with a "slip-in" pumper.

1972 — The Tiny Tonka line still has the aerial ladder as No. 675 and the kit No. 830. The pumper does not appear in the catalogue. No. 1065, the Fire Chiefs car still is in the catalogue. No. 1255 is still the "Super-Thrust" pumper. The major change in this year was a new aerial ladder. It is rear-mounted ladder like the apparatus that was popular from that era. The truck has dual tires and an ABS ladder. The cab is an "open-cab". The overall length is 24 5/16", 8 1/8" high and 6" wide. The catalogue number was 2960. The snorkel is still available as number 2950.

The catalogue for this year announced it was their "Silver Anniversary." Twenty-five years of toy manufacturing.

1973 — A new line, the Tonka "Gigglers" had a fire truck as part of a set of toys. The Firecar set had a Fire Chief, Fireman and Firecar. These toys doubled as finger puppets. The catalogue number was 5530. The old number 675 is still in the catalogue. The kit 830 is still there too. The Super-Thrust is still No. 125. Snorkel No. 2950 is still available and so is the rear-mount aerial, still No. 2960. The Smokey Bear kit is still available as 5035.

1974 — The Tiny Tonka is still available as No. 675. The kit is still available as No. 830. The Super-Thrust pumper has been renumbered as 1256. The pumper stores water and has a pump and hose that actually work. Numbers 2950 and 2960 are still in the catalogue.

1975 — Number 6998 is called the "Funny Firefighter". It consists of a set of "peek-a-boo" puppets as Fire Chief and Firefighter. The puppets come out of the vehicle. Bell rings when buttons are pushed. The vehicle has little "fire chiefs car" on the inside of the main vehicle. The main vehicle was 8¼" long, 6¼" high and 6" wide.

Numbers 595, kit No. 830 and 675 are still in the catalogue. Number 999, a Rescue Van is in the inventory of this year as a separate entry. This vehicle is painted red-orange. 5" long, 2½" high and 2 1/8" wide. Pumper number 1256 is recommended to be matched with Rescue Van "999" or Rescue Wagoneer number 1995. Rescue Wagoneer number 1995 has a fold-down tailgate for loading victims, simulated flasher and siren. The vehicle says Tonka on the bottom side panels and "Rescue" on the roof. The siren is located in the middle of the roof of the cab, projecting from the "box" used as the ambulance area. The overall length is 9¼", 4 7/8" high and 3 5/8" wide. Numbers 2950 and 2960 still available.

The first Mighty Tonkas with emergency service implication are in this catalogue. The number 3875 is a Rescue vehicle patterned after an ambulance.

1976 — Good old numbers 595 and 675 are in this catalogue. Kit number 830 is still there too. A new kit appears in this year with the appearance of kit 973 — The Community Set. This kit had a fire apparatus among a mobile crime lab, a sanitation truck and a wrecker/tow truck. Number 999 rescue van is still there too. Number 1256 and rescue van 1995 still in. 1950 and 2960 still in the series. 6998, the Funny Firefighter still in the catalogue also.

1977 — Standbys 595, 675 and kit 830 still available. The 973 Community set is still in the catalogue. Number 4997, the TONKA FIRE HAT appears in the series. No dimensions were in the listing, but they were shipped 18 to a shipper, the weight was 13 lbs. They appear to be molded of lightweight plastic. They had a head-band to fit any size head.

A new "Fire/Rescue Kit" appears as catalogue number 1958. This kit included the 1256 pumper, the new 1962 aerial ladder and a rescue vehicle. The kit was 22¾" long, 10 7/8" high and 4½" wide. The new aerial ladder was designated catalogue number 1962. This new modification was center mounted with a simulated instrument panel. Cab-over design. 21¾" long, 5 3/16" high and 4 3/8" wide. Rescue vehicle 1995 is still in the catalogue. Snorkel 2950 and ladder 2960 are still available.

The Tonka "MITES" were introduced this year. The first fire apparatus was the aerial ladder No. 143. No dimensions given.

1978 — Number 830 kit is still in. 595 and 675 aerial are there too. Number 999 rescue is still there. The 4997 Tonka helmet is still available. The old 1256 pumper has been renumbered 1856. The number 23 appears on the catalogue photograph on the door of the truck. The 1962 aerial still in.

The new number for this year is the 1386 Fire/Rescue truck. This is a conventional cab truck with a "slip-in" type pumper. The hose reel is molded on the back and the head of the pump box. The number 606 appears on the side of the apparatus on the decal. Pumper 2950 is still in, as well as aerial 2960.

The MITE Tonkas include a pumper numbered 183 and an aerial numbered 143. No details given on dimensions. Another "hook and ladder" was numbered 197.

1979 — The 1979 catalogue was drastically changed from the previous years. The toys were illustrated, but very few details were available.

There was a "Community Set" with number 279; the Fire Truck that was otherwise labeled as Truck No. 206 in previous catalogues. Kit 830 was still available and Aerial ladder 675 is still represented. In the Compact series there was a 1386 Fire/Rescue vehicle. The aerial ladder marked as catalogue number 1935 is identified as "new". This aerial has the numeral 3 on the side of the cab and the trailer. This truck came with two firefighters also. The dimensions appear to be in the range of 20-22" length. The 2950 Snorkel and 2960 Aerial is still in the catalogue also. It is also interesting to note in the rear of the catalogue that the term "Snorkel" was used with the permission of the Snorkel Fire Apparatus Company.

Tonka "Builders" came out this year with a Playset "Fire Station" that was identified as "ENGINE HOUSE 23". These kits were snap-fitted and came in assortments.

1980 — The 1980 catalogue was also very slight in details. Kit 830 is still illustrated. The Fire/Rescue vehicle is labeled as number 1386. The aerial ladder in the Play People series is still identified as No. 1935. Numbers 2950 and 2960 still in the series. "Builder's" kit number 5099 still includes the Engine House 23.

1981 — The number 830 set for ages 2 to 8 years old is still in the catalogue. In the material we received to research this catalogue review, the first 20 years were all xeroxed copies so colors were difficult to determine. But the 1981 version was in glorious color and it could be determined that the 830 kit components are red metal with yellow plastic parts. The 1935 aerial ladder is described as being for ages 3 to 10 years old. It too had yellow plastic components. It is also interesting to note in this catalogue that the two firefighters that come with the kit, one is white and the other is black. This probably represents the realization that affirmative action aspects in society also impacted the toy industry.

Also this catalogue gave the first dimensions of the 1935 aerial ladder. It is described as 24" in length, 5 7/8" in height. The 2950 Snorkel is also shown with yellow plastic parts. The overall dimensions of the 2950 unit was 19 5/8" in length, 9 7/8" in height and 6 3/8" in width. The 2960 aerial does not appear in this catalogue.

1982 — The 830 kit does not appear this year. The 1935 Aerial with two play people is there . . . and that's it.

Summary — This review of the catalogue is cursory at best. I have tried to give you a good idea of the sequence that Tonka introduced their fire service related toys. If any of you collectors out there have additional information that modifies any of these observations, please let us know. We took this information from some xerox copies that may or may not represent all of the data.

I think that it is safe to say that Tonka has produced millions of fire truck toys that have thrilled and excited many a young child. They made an excellent toy that stood up to abuse and love equally. If you can find some of the earlier ones in mint condition, they are an excellent addition to a collection.

A Plastic Scratch-built version of a 1915 British
Fire Truck with a front mount Fire Pump. The
crew sat on the back of the truck. This version
is about 5" long.

It doesn't take much to convert many of the
scale cars into a "Fire Vehicle". This is a John
Ford kit that was painted red, some decals taken
from another kit and the red lights and siren added to make it a Fire Car. The overall length is
about 5.5".

This is a model of British Two Ton Comer Truck
with firefighting equipment that was designed to
put out fires on the battleground. The toy was
fabricated from a plastic model kit. The overall
length is about 5.5".

166

GLICKMAN TOY.

MFG. UNKNOWN, made in Japan in 1958. Made of pressed tin. No serial number. Approximately 7" long. The motor is friction powered. When the vehicle moves, the motor pistons move up and down.

MATCHBOX (LESNEY), made in England in 1974. The toy is die cast metal with some plastic parts. The serial number on the toy is K50-53. The overall dimensions of the toy are 4¼".

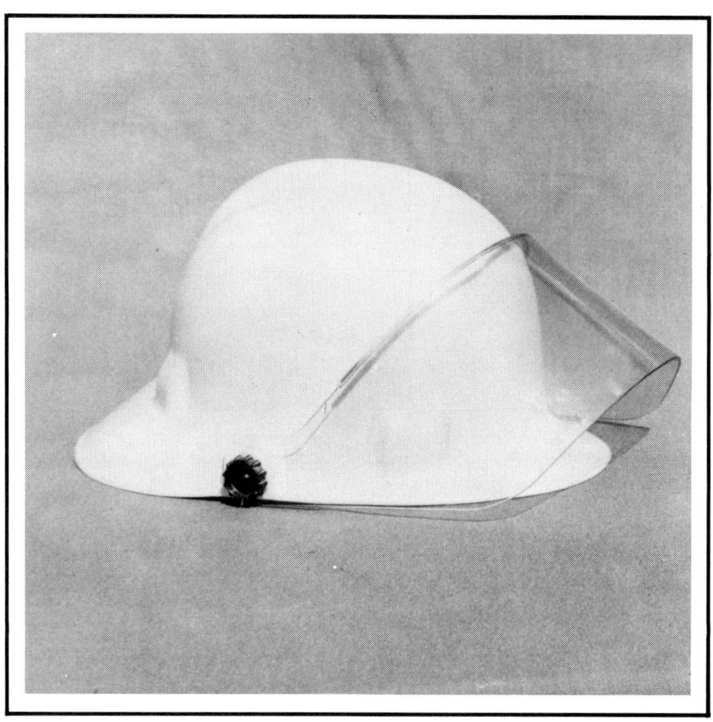

A lot of people don't know that Ray and I got into the publishing business because of our success in raising money by designing fire helmets. This is the current helmet designed and manufactured by Phenix Technology. It is called the "First-Due Firefighter." Our first helmet design work was performed for a company called American Sports Company in Gardena. As a result of a difference of opinion in helmet design we moved on and formed our own company, Phenix Technology. For about 12 years we made helmets and sold them exclusively for Western Fire Equipment as the "Firecraft" Helmet. Recently, we have changed that relationship and now manufacture helmets for direct sales.

The way we got into the helmet business was our collection. Ray and I and several others were looking at the various helmets on display and trying to decide what helmet was the world's "best". We have over 500 helmets in the collection so the debate got heated . . . at any rate our first design was to come out of that discussion. We estimate that we have now sold close to 100,000 helmets. Most of the modern helmet manufacturers in this country have chosen to come up with designs based on this "European" style profile . . . perhaps imitation is still the best form of flattery.

SEAVER TOY COMPANY. Made in the U.S.A. in Burbank, California in the early 1950's. It was made of wood and had an overall dimension of 21½". A pull toy.

MANHATTEN "8". Reportedly one of the first
Steamers in their NYFD.

BROOKLIN MODELS, made in England in 1980.
It is a die cast metal toy. The markings on the toy
are "For-D (9). It is manufactured to the 1/43 scale
and is a very detailed piece. It is patterned after a
1940 Ford sedan that was uesed as a rescue vehicle.

**This HELMET FRONTPIECE was reportedly
worn on** by Fire Chief John Decker

No 1
NAVAL TORPEDO STATION

MODERN FIRE FIGHTING APPARATUS
IMPROVED MOTOR DRIVEN AERIAL LADDER TRUCK - 1921 PERIOD

MODERN FIRE FIGHTING APPARATUS
FIRST MOTORIZED HOOK & LADDER TRUCK — 1915 PERIOD

ENERGOL
ENERGOL
visco-static
LONGLIFE
ENERGOL

DEALERS

The following list shows dealers of various kinds of toys. All have toy fire engines, both antique and new, foreign and domestic. Each has a catalogue available. We would be grateful to know of any other dealers that should be included in this section that deal in toy fire trucks.

Holland Hobby Sales
Postbus 6747
6503 GE NIJME
The Netherlands

Roberts Company
P.O. Box 77 COCH
Wayland, Mass. 01778

Autofanatics Ltd.
P.O. Box 1091
Studio City, CA 91604

Marque Products
635 Paularino Ave.
Costa Mesa, CA 92626

Sinclair's Auto Miniatures
3831 West 12th Street
Erie, Pa. 16505

Copy Cars
P.O. Box 481
Tustin, CA 92680

Mini-Wheels of Midland
P.O. Box 7414
Midlands, Texas 79703

James Wieland
Miniature Auto Sales
E2 Tapping Reeve
Litchfield, Conn. 06759

Firefighters Toys
Attn.: Chuck Ford
875 Durham St.
La Habra, CA 90631

Daves Model Toys
416 S. Rollins Road
Catonsville, Md. 21228

Maryland & Gils Fire Station
Road 3, Box 83
Catskill, N.Y. 12414

Toys for Collectors
P.O. Box 1406
Attelboro Falls, Mass. 02763

Chuck Satterfield Gifts
1813 South Quincy
Burlington, VA 22204

Miniature Toys, Inc.
P.O. Drawer E
1517 East Main Street (Rear)
Westboro, Mass. 01881

Polk Model Crafts
  & Hobbies, Inc.
346 Bergen Ave.
Jersey City, N.J. 07304

TOY FIRE TRUCK INVENTORY

MAKE	MODEL	ERA	PURCHASE COST	REMARKS

MAKE	MODEL	ERA	PURCHASE COST	REMARKS

TOY FIRE TRUCK INVENTORY

MAKE	MODEL	ERA	PURCHASE COST	REMARKS

TOY FIRE TRUCK INVENTORY

MAKE	MODEL	ERA	PURCHASE COST	REMARKS

INDEX
VOLUME II

SCALE MODELS

SCALE MODELS

TOYS for COLLECTORS
P.O. BOX 1406, ATTLEBORO FALLS,
MASS. 02763

For Illustrated Catalogue
Send $3.00